MODELING CLA...

COMBAT AIRCRAFT

COMPILED BY MARK THOMPSON

KALMBACH BOOKS

Printed in Canada

03 04 05 06 07 08 09 10 11 12   10 9 8 7 6 5 4 3 2 1

Visit our Web site at http://kalmbachbooks.com
Secure online ordering available

Publisher's Cataloging-in-Publication
(Provided by Quality Books, Inc.)

Modeling classic combat aircraft / compiled by Mark
  Thompson.
    p. cm.
    ISBN 0-89024-394-8

    1. Airplanes, Military—Models.   I. Thompson, Mark
(Mark O.), 1946-

    TL770.M63 2003   623.7'46'0228
                            QBI03-200733

Art director: Kristi Ludwig
Book design: Mark Watson

The material in this book has previously appeared as articles in *FineScale Modeler* Magazine. Most are reprinted in their entirety and may include an occasional reference to an item elsewhere in the same issue or in a previous issue of the magazine.

CONTENTS

Building Yeager's Mustang

MODELING "GLAMOROUS GLEN III" IN 1/32 SCALE

Chuck Yeager's "Glamorous Glen III," made from the old Hasegawa kit, looks great posed with a figure, goggles, Air Medal, and a map of World War II-era Europe. *Photo by Jim Forbes.*

The North American P-51D Mustang, the most potent and versatile WWII fighter jet, having destroyed more enemy aircraft in the air than any other fighter in Europe, is a popular modeling subject. When I decided to model the Mustang, I chose Hasegawa's 1/32 scale rendition, which was first released in the summer of 1973 at a list price of $4.50. It reflects the state of the kit maker's art 28 years ago—how things have changed. But it's still basically a good kit with a pretty accurate outline and decent fit.

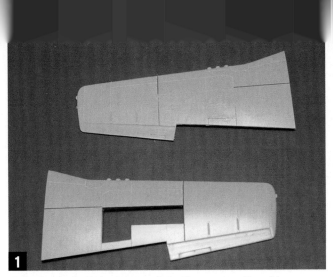

1

Pat glued stretched sprue into the unusually wide recessed lines of the upper wing halves.

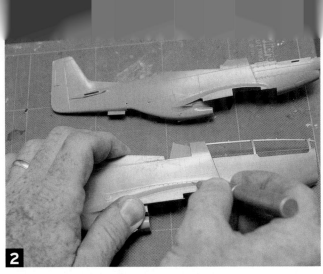

2

While Pat poked holes in the wing fairing to represent rivets, he kept a Tamiya 1/48 scale fuselage handy as a rivet and panel line reference.

By Pat Hawkey
Photos by the author

However, like all early 1/32 scale kits, it lacks detail we now take for granted. The cockpit, wheel wells, landing gear, exposed Merlin engine, guns, and ammo bays are basic. Unfortunately, in this big scale, basic really doesn't cut it. This model is also covered with tiny rivet heads and raised panel lines, which is not what most of us want to see when approaching a big natural-metal project. You're going to have to work a bit to get a really good representation of a P-51, but isn't a fine Mustang model worth it?

The year 2000 re-issue of the Hasegawa Mustang features decals for "Glamorous Glen III," the airplane flown by (then) Captain Chuck Yeager. Otherwise, the kit is unchanged from the original.

When the opportunity arose to build this particular model for *FineScale Modeler*, I was ready. I'd built the same kit for a client a couple years before, and while everybody who saw it seemed to like it, it was built to some specs I didn't agree with. After building a big Mustang for somebody the way they wanted it, I was itching to do one the way I thought it should be done! Here we go.

Flaps, down! When a Merlin-powered Mustang's engine is shut down, so is the hydraulic pump, so the hydraulically activated flaps and wheel covers slowly drop to the full down position. So, if you are modeling a D Mustang at rest, the flaps and doors should be down. While I was cutting the flaps from the wings, I also separated the elevators from the stabilizers. Instead of using a saw, I scribed repeatedly along the hinge lines with a needle chucked in a pin vise, then wiggled the flap or elevator until the joint began to give. After a few swipes with a No. 11 blade the parts were free. I glued the flaps and elevator halves together and set them aside.

The elevators and rudder are marred by overdone "fabric detail" (which looks like burlap). These should be as smooth as the rest of the airplane. I scraped and sanded the coarse "detail" away. At this early stage I also installed the left gun bay doors into the wing, using liberal amounts of gap-filling super glue on the inside surface.

New panel lines. My next job was to re-scribe all surface detail. I scribed new lines right alongside the raised lines before sanding them down. For reasons we can only guess at, Hasegawa chose a few panel lines at random to engrave deeply. I filled these with stretched sprue secured with liquid cement, **1**. Were I to do it again, I'd rely more on gap-filling super glue. Re-scribing the sprue-filled lines proved problematic, with the sprue coming loose in places.

The raised lines that are provided are fairly accurate in location, but I also relied on Tamiya's superb 1/48 scale P-51D interpretation as a guide to scribing. For the most part, I used my chucked needle with a drafting eraser shield as a straight-edge, **2**. An eraser shield (available in art-supply stores) is a thin metal sheet that protects pencil artwork while erasing errors.

Scribing the wings and stabilizers was straightforward, but the fuselage, with its prominent rivets and fasteners, was a bit more involved. The fairings that join wings and stabilizers to the fuselage are attached on the real airplane with noticeable rivets—that's a lot of holes to be poked! The recessed fasteners around the nose panels are especially evident on real P-51s, and these I represented (for the sake of speed) by a poke of the needle followed by a twist of a No. 70 drill bit. In retrospect, I should've given the wing fairing rivets a twist of a small drill bit as well.

Sand, prime, smooth. When the scribing operation was complete, I sanded everything smooth with a combination of medium-grit sanding stick and 400-grit sandpaper. Fortunately, the raised detail provided is fairly light and not difficult to remove.

The exterior got its first of many primer coats at this stage, **3**. A lot of glitches appeared under the primer, and I re-sanded or filled crooked

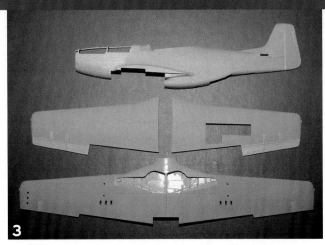

3 Pat tinted his gray primer with paint (here green) to make it more obvious against gray plastic. He masked areas he didn't want primed with thin strips of tape.

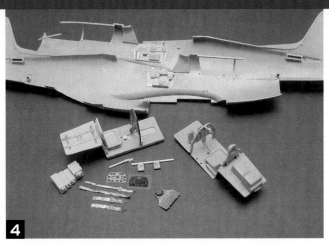

4 Verlinden's unpainted interior (left) is better than the Hasegawa representation, but it still has faults.

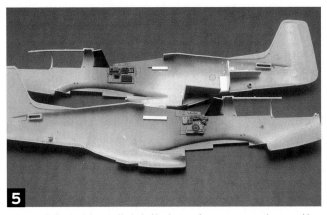

5 The painted side wall detail shows improvement over the kit parts. The fuselage halves are ready to be brought together. The white strips will hold the radio deck.

6 The cockpit floor, seat, stick, and instrument panel will be inserted from below before the wing is attached to the fuselage.

lines and missed corners with gap-filling super glue. Then I sanded and primed again. There would be lots more priming and sanding before this model was ready for paint.

Department of the interior. Verlinden's detail kit No. 787, a combination of resin and photoetched parts, copper wire, and a celluloid instrument face piece, was my choice for the cockpit interior, 4. It replaced virtually the entire Hasegawa cockpit array, and saved a lot of time. However, there were some minor problems. Certain items seemed to be a bit overscale, especially on the left side wall where not all the bits have enough room to squeeze in. The carburetor hot air control lever was squeezed right out the project, in fact. The seat belts and buckles look

to me closer to 1/24 scale than 1/32. I used the buckles, but substituted cut and wrinkled strips of lead foil for the too- rigid photoetched straps.

A photoetched instrument panel coaming is provided, and the installation of this piece caused some problems. Trimming as per the instructions removed too much of the kit's coaming. I discovered this problem only after I had the instrument panel secured to the floor in the notches provided. Test fitting quickly showed the panel to be too far aft (closer to the seat) in relation to the coaming. I broke it loose and installed it as a separate item, having to compromise on location. To set it in far enough and allow room for the under-coaming instrument lights, the attached rudder pedals would've

been too far away for a 1/32 scale Capt. Yeager to reach.

Closing in. I determined the smartest building sequence would be to build the fuselage so the cockpit floor/seat assembly could be inserted from below later, 5. This would avoid potential damage resulting from handling this assembly. Before securing the fuselage halves I partially boxed in the tail wheel well, 6. I didn't bother with a rear wall—you can't see back in there anyway.

The kit comes with an upper cowl panel designed to be removed to view the engine, and not surprisingly, getting a good tight fit here wasn't easy. I super glued a section at a time, using clamps to hold the panel flush with the fuselage.

Two other fuselage spots that

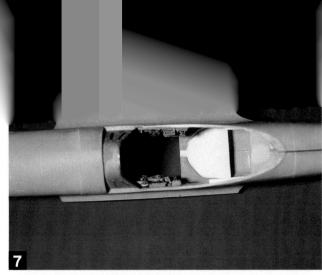

7 Looking down into the assembled fuselage reveals the roof added to the radiator interior. Also seen just behind the wing leading edge is epoxy putty blended to get the desired smooth upper fuselage contour.

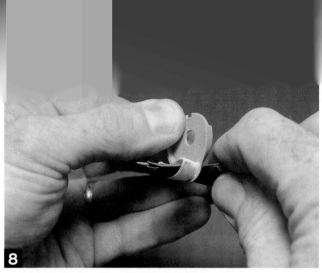

8 Pat forces 400-grit sandpaper with a straight pin into the corners of the carburetor intake.

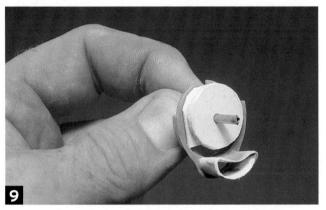

9 The propeller shaft and carburetor intake are ready to install in the nose.

10 Matching the curve of the spinner to the curve of the fuselage was the priority in getting the nosepiece in place. Note the styrene shim needed to fill a gap.

needed attention were the ventral radiator scoop and the nose carburetor intake; both are just open holes into the model. I made a roof for the radiator intake out of .030" sheet styrene and filled the gaps and cracks inside with epoxy putty, **7**. It was a little tricky getting files and sanding sticks into the confined area to work it smooth.

The carburetor intake was more involved as there was nothing there to start with but a hole. I carved and sanded a small block of balsa to the size and shape of what the interior of the intake would be. With what I hoped would be a usable master, I dusted off my trusty Mattel Vac-U-Form and a sheet of .040" styrene. This is thicker than the machine is designed to accept, and I had to

clamp the plastic holder tight with a small pair of visegrips. The first draw was a good one. This was happy news, as my balsa master didn't survive the removal from my new part.

I glued my scoop interior behind the intake opening of kit part C13 and sliced off the rear end. I didn't get a perfect fit where my part met the kit part. Intake interiors are very smooth places and this was another very tight place to get a seamless look. I dabbed thick super glue into the gaps and cracks and when dry, following it with 400-grit sandpaper wrapped around a long straight pin, **8**. This got me into the tight corners and worked well. I painted the inside silver and glued a flat black backing piece to the rear end to give some illusion of depth.

Talkin' 'bout shaft. Since I wasn't going to install the engine, and the engine contained the propeller shaft, I had to improvise. I took 1/16" brass tube, cut a 1" length, and stuck it through a 5/8" disc of heavy sheet stock, **9**. I centered and cemented this in the back of part C13, using the spinner as an alignment guide. When this was set, I again used the round of the spinner, matched to the round of the nose, as a guide to get C13 correctly positioned to the front of the airplane, **10**. This was not a tight fit. When I had the front end of the fuselage blended in, primed, re-scribed and sanded some more, I installed the interior and focused on the wings.

Wingman. The right gun bay was to be displayed open. As with the

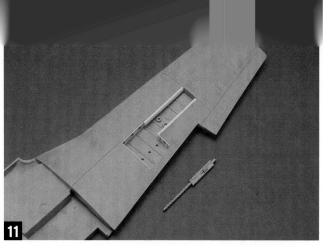

11 Pat inserted styrene walls in the gun bay, and substituted a better .50-cal. machine gun from the Hasegawa F-86.

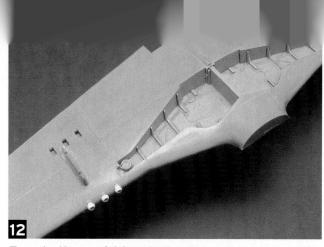

12 To make the gun fairings better, Pat replaced them with styrene tubing.

13 Using a photo enlarged to 1/32 scale, Pat determined that the kit drop tanks were too small.

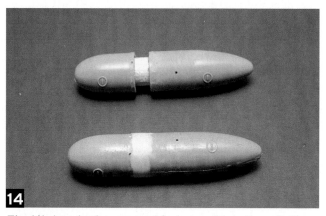

14 The kit drop tanks were cut in two and lengthened. The tank on top shows the wooden dowel used to maintain correct length. The bottom tank has had the gap filled with epoxy putty.

cockpit, Hasegawa provided a very simplified version of what was supposed to be in there. I added sheet styrene walls, tightened the ammo bay with Evergreen square stock and replaced the guns with a trio of better-shaped examples from a 1/32 scale Hasegawa F-86, **11**. Unfortunately it was only very late in the game that I discovered the ammo belt leading to the inboard gun ended up forward of the gun's breech. The fix would be to change the angle of the belt guide—no quick and easy job and the clock was ticking. I chose to live with the goof.

A sore spot on nearly all P-51 kits is the shape of the gun fairings. The top/bottom wing split puts a seam through the fairings that's hard to clean up, and in the case of this particular kit, the edges were not sharply defined. I shaved and sanded off what

came molded on the wings and replaced them with rounded segments of ⅛" styrene tubing, **12**. Because the leading edges of the wings aren't as sharp as they should be (no true laminar flow wing here) I didn't get the characteristic top and bottom bulge of the real thing. Still, it was a better representation than Hasegawa's.

Expanding tanks. Photos show "Glamorous Glen III" with the pressed-paper drop tanks late in the war. The kit tanks looked stubby to me. I enlarged a side-view photo of a P-51 carrying paper tanks to 1/32 scale (using a kit wheel as my sizing guide) and, matching a tank half to the photo, found them to be 5mm too short, **13**. I glued them together, then sawed them in half, spaced the halves to the correct 83mm length with dowel epoxied in place. Then I filled the resulting gap with epoxy

putty and shaved and sanded the tanks smooth, **14**. I chose not to try to represent the ribbing of the front and back ends, as photos show the ribs to be very faint. I replaced the prominent pair of encircling bands with strip stock. The location of these bands was set by the pylon, but I discovered too late that the kit racks were also too short. Oh, well.

I used straight pins to mount the tanks to their wing racks. The plumbing to get the fuel from the drop tanks into the wing tanks was all external and fairly prominent. I drilled holes into the tanks and into the wings where the lines needed to go, then cut and bent wire to the proper length and angles to represent hoses, **15**. I wanted these perfect, so that when it came time to install them for good when everything was silver and easily scratched, they'd pop

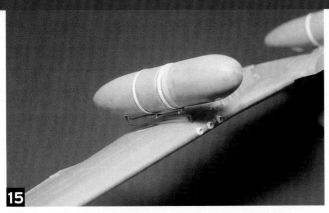

15 The modified drop tanks and exterior plumbing are test-fitted before painting.

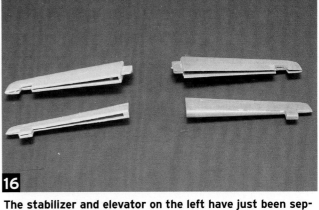

16 The stabilizer and elevator on the left have just been separated. Pat thinned the interior trailing edges of the stabilizer and built up the leading edge of the elevator (right).

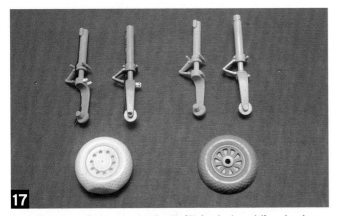

17 Landing gear improvements (left) include adding brake lines and tow rings to the struts. Hasegawa's incorrect spoked inner-wheel half on the right is superfluous if you use the True Details resin wheels.

REFERENCES
357th Fighter Group James Roeder, Squadron/Signal Publications, Carrollton, Texas, 2000
P-51 Mustang in Detail and Scale Part 2 Bert Kinzey, Squadron/Signal Publications, Carrollton, Texas, 1997
Pursue and Destroy Leonard "Kit" Carson, Sentry Books Inc., Granada Hills, California, 1978
Walk Around P-51D Larry Davis, Squadron/Signal Publications, Carrollton, Texas, 1996
The Yoxford Boys Merle C. Olmstead, Aero Publishers Inc., Fallbrook, California, 1971

SOURCES
Cockpit set Verlinden Productions, 811 Lone Star Drive 63366 O'Fallon, MO 63366, 636-379-0077, www.verlinden-productions.com
True Details wheels and vaccuum-formed canopy Squadron Products, 1115 Crowley Drive, Carrollton, TX 75011-5010, 972-242-8663, www.squadron.com
Light lenses M.V. Products, P.O. Box 6622, Orange, CA 92863-6622
Parafilm M sold by Testor Corp., 620 Buckbee St., Rockford, IL 61104-4891, 815-962-6654, www.testors.com

right into their holes without fuss.

With the wing and tank assemblies just about done, I joined wing to fuselage and worked on getting the separate flaps to fit. I'd built up the open forward areas of the flaps with heavy styrene stock and epoxy putty then sanded the top leading edge round. This fit against a much-thinned trailing edge of upper wing halves. There followed a lot of fitting, adjusting, and re-fitting of flaps to wings to get a close to perfect fit and the 47-degree full-down angle. (Paragon makes resin flaps for this kit which I used on the previous Mustang, but I preferred to use my own the second time around.)

Once I was satisfied with the fit I superglued the flaps in place. I thought painting them while attached to the airplane was preferable to putting them on afterward

and risking a glue mark on the aluminum finish. I also glued the elevators to the stabilizers, **16**.

Grind the gears. I wanted the landing gear to fit well the first time after the model was painted, so these were dealt with way before the paint flew. The gear itself is good, but basic. I cleaned up mold marks and added brake lines and tow rings. The oleo scissors are thick and could use replacement, but I didn't bother. The kit wheels are wrong in that they show spokes on both sides. Spokes faced outboard while holes faced inboard on the real airplane. Fortunately True Details came to the rescue with their resin wheels (set No. 32001), **17**. I did sand away some of the bulged bottom of the tires to lessen the under-inflated look, however. The wheel wells are typically very basic, and I drew the line here. I

decided that I'd leave them as they came and discourage anybody from turning "Glen" upside down to inspect them.

Canopy, anyone? The windscreen is molded with part of the upper fuselage and joins at panel lines all around. This is the smart approach from a modeler's point of view. The sliding section on the other hand comes as two separate pieces; the frame that rides the fuselage and the clear hood. This presents two problems. The clear piece is joined to its sprue on the edge, and that's going to show. Problem two is that gluing the canopy to the frame for a perfect fit and a solid hold, without allowing any glue to show, is a challenge. There's just not much surface there to join.

After several attempts to glue and touch up the joints, I became frustrated and crunched it in a fist.

18

"Glamorous Glen III" is moments away from becoming silver. The cockpit, gun bay and all pre-painted areas are covered, leaving only the fine sanded airframe showing.

19

A combination of Post-it notes and Parafilm M are used to mask off fuselage and control surfaces prior to painting tinted silver on the wings.

Fortunately for me I had a second kit handy, and started again. My only suggestion would be to polish the clear piece beforehand and be ultra-careful securing it to the frame. (Only when all this work was done did I discover Squadron Products has come out with vacuum-formed canopies for both standard and Dallas hood Mustangs in 1/32 scale!)

I masked and painted the inside of the windscreen frame flat black; in this scale, leaving shiny clear plastic inside there just wouldn't do. Masking the exterior windscreen panels was tedious, as the raised lines indicating their location are very faint. Slow and careful cutting of Scotch Magic tape did the job. With the windscreen secure I wet-sanded the model one last time with 1000-grit sandpaper.

Aluminum finish. Since I needed to apply the aluminum finish to as smooth a surface as possible, I masked and painted the rudder, invasion stripes, antiglare panel, and ring around the nose first. (I painted the nose ring yellow and planned to separate the red checks from the decal sheet and apply them separately when the time came; I never trust decals to fit compound curved surfaces.) When the paint was completely dry, I removed the masks. This way the areas to be painted aluminum had no overspray from the other colors—just a smooth plastic

surface, ideal for a natural-metal finish. Now I had to mask the pre-painted areas to protect them from the aluminum color, **18**.

My aluminum finish of choice is good old Testor Model Master Chrome Silver thinned with Floquil Dio-sol, which helps it dry faster. I like this paint because I can put it on thick and heavy enough to fill and hide many of the fine sanding scratches that other metallics will highlight. The down side is that it takes a while to dry; in fact, I'm not convinced it ever dries completely. For this reason, I make sure I have a "handle"—an area on the model that I can hold without marring the finish. In this case, it is the invasion-striped radiator.

After letting the paint dry for a couple days, I masked the fuselage, flaps, and ailerons and airbrushed the wing with a mix of Chrome Silver and white to produce the painted-wing look peculiar to P-51Ds—the wings actually were painted with aluminum lacquer at the factory to seal panels and smooth the surface of the laminar-flow design.

Next I added a few drops of blue to fresh Chrome Silver and sprayed this on a few panels to change the tones. I masked with a combination of Post-it notes for flat, straight segments and Parafilm M for curves, **19**. I keep a test wing or fuselage handy to show me how different the new mix is

going to look against the base color before I commit paint to the model. I don't want a patchwork-quilt look; the differences on the real airplane are subtle. The only panels that are noticeably different than the rest are those around the exhaust stacks. Here I mixed a bit of black with Chrome Silver.

Ready to decal. Decal adhesive can mar Testor Chrome Silver, so I gave this model a few coats of Testor Glosscote. This kills the chrome gleam, but I didn't want a glimmering finish anyway. More important, it provided a barrier between the decals and the silver paint.

The decals went on without any problem. The black ID bands came from Expert's Choice black decal stock. I also cut tiny ovals in this black decal with a scribing template (Verlinden Productions has one) to simulate the inspection openings in the tops of the flaps. The flap-degree indicator on the left flap was made from a block of white decal stock with black hashmarks cut and added on top.

"Sludge wash." With the decals dry, I mixed a very dilute solution of water, dish soap, and acrylic flat black (about a 50/30/20 mix) to make a wash. The dish soap is important as it reduces the adhesion of the black paint. I applied this wash over all the aluminum surfaces except the wing—photos I studied showed

Pat Hawkey's finished model of the "Glamorous Glen III" looks ready for combat.

nearly invisible panel lines on the painted wings of real P-51s. (I am firmly against "bringing out detail" when this detail is not seen on the real thing.) When dry, I wiped the black wash off with a damp rag, leaving the panel lines and rivet depressions darkened. Once all the black wash was removed from where it didn't belong, the model got a final sealing shot of Glosscote.

Final assembly. I immediately installed the landing gear to keep the belly from coming in contact with any surfaces and getting scratched. Next I installed the drop tanks.

I used a suitably sized lens from M.V. Products for the landing light in the left gear bay. You can also find M.V. lenses in colors and use them for the underwing red, green, and amber ID lights. I also added the big center landing gear door actuators from stretched sprue and styrene tube.

I kept "weathering"—though weather has little to do with it—to a minimum. I put some black chalk pastel streaks under the fuselage gas cap and dabbed Polly Scale Oily Black very lightly on the tops of the wings near the forward roots and around the gun bays—areas oil, grease, and dirty boots were likely to tread.

The finished model represents a little more than 100 (closely counted) hours of hands-on work. Were Hasegawa to do this kit again to today's standards, I'll bet you would get the same finished result in half the time. Can you imagine how well a truly great, 1/32 scale model of the P-51D would sell?

Great solutions for vexing problems

Pat used a couple of interesting tricks in finishing his Mustang, including this method for painting the spinner.

Painting straight stripes on a compound curve like the Mustang spinner is difficult. Pat wrapped masking tape around the spinner and roughly drew the location of the stripe with pencil. He then removed the tape, laid it flat, then refined the pencil line with a draftsman's compass.

Using the compass with a cutting blade, Pat cut out a strip to mask the edges of the yellow stripe. A pair of dividers is used to ensure even width all around. The gap between the taped edges is filled with additional masking material, and then the red paint is applied.

Removing the masking tape reveals a perfectly painted stripe.

The muzzles of the .50s were represented with sections of styrene tube stretched the same way you heat and stretch sprue. A little trial and error led to the proper diameters needed, and these were cut guillotine-style with a single-edge razor blade.

CHAPTER TWO

Detailing a B-25D strafer in 1/48 scale

CONVERSION TIPS FOR MONOGRAM'S MITCHELL

Seemingly defying gravity, Paul Budzik's Mitchell shows off more than just detail. Brass tubes mounted on the propeller and inside the engines allow the props to spin with just a little breeze.

The B-25 Mitchell has always been one of my favorite bombers; something about its lines, I guess. The Mitchell was at its best as a low-level bomber and strafer against Japanese shipping and military installations in World War II. Early versions had only a single forward-firing machine gun in the nose, so crews added firepower for the strafing mission. As many as eight .50-cal. machine guns were bolted onto and into the nose of the Mitchell.

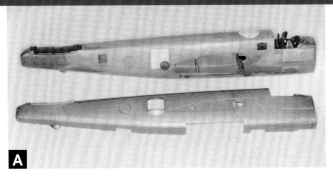

A

B

C

D

E

By Paul Budzik

I wanted a model of a gun-nosed strafer for my 1/48 scale collection, so I backdated Monogram's late B-25J into a D model. I could have reached the same result with the Revell B-25B kit, but I decided instead to use a few parts from Revell on the better-detailed Monogram kit.

Fuselage Modifications. Monogram's interior detail is outstanding. I added full seat backs and headrests to the kit seats using .020" sheet styrene. I enlarged and filled the waist gun positions, upper turret opening, entrance hatches, and nose gear door with sheet styrene and sanded them smooth. My model would be posed gear up on a stand, so I didn't have to work on the landing gear. I also closed the bomb bay doors but added .030" styrene strips to the center line of each door to fill the gap. I cut slightly oversize window openings and filled them with clear sheet acrylic, (**A**). After sanding and polishing, the "glass" areas would be masked before painting.

After painting the interior, I placed Monogram's pilot in the copilot's seat and a figure from Monogram's B-26 Marauder in the pilot's seat (**B**).

I cemented the fuselage halves, then drilled a hole through the top and bottom on the center line just aft of the bomb bay doors to hold a rod for a stand. Mounting the end of the rod in a vise helps to align the wings

and tail plane on the fuselage. I added the tail plane first, then removed the late-model's tail-gunner fairing and filled the opening with sheet styrene (**C**). The new clear tail blister is shaped and polished acrylic rod.

I used the kit's clear nose piece for the new gun nose. I filled the original holes and added acrylic inside to support the new gun barrels. After drilling four new holes (slightly larger in diameter than the barrels), I attached the nose to the fuselage (**D**). The exterior framing was sanded smooth, replaced with strips of Bare-Metal Foil, and painted over with the rest of the fuselage.

I located the new opening for the top turret by striking an average dimension from several scale drawings which differed in its location. Monogram's turret interior is one of the best I have ever seen, but the clear bubble seems too big. I fashioned a master from acrylic rod and vacuum-formed over it with thin sheet acrylic (**E**). I made new gun barrels for the nose and turret from .040" brass wire.

A

B

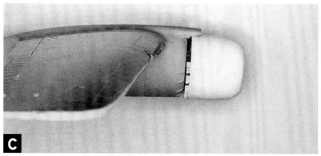

C

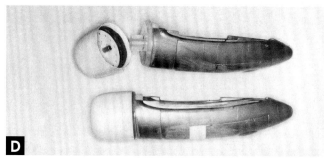

D

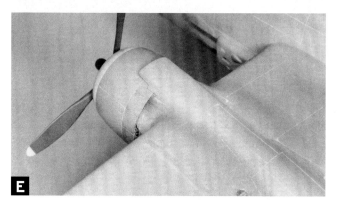

E

REFERENCE
Warpath Across the Pacific Lawrence J. Hickey, International Research and Publishing Corp., Boulder, Colorado, 1984

Engines, Cowls, and Nacelles. The gear cases of Monogram's engines looked too small, so I modified Revell B-25 engines. I began by assembling the two cylinder rows, then chucked the gear case in a miniature lathe and drilled out the center. I attached a brass tube (long enough to extend beyond the rear row of cylinders) with super glue. The tube allows me to center the engine assemblies through the remaining modifications. I mounted the engine in a lathe and ground away the molded-on ignition harness and pushrods. My new ignition harness was made from brass tubing and fine copper wire, while the new pushrods were cut from stainless-steel wire (**A**).

My references indicate the cowls were round, but the rear of Monogram's were irregular ovals. I made new cowlings by vacuum-forming .060" sheet styrene over masters turned from thick-walled PVC pipe (**B**). I then trimmed each cowl to length and scribed panel lines. Next I fashioned a couple of styrene disks for engine mounts; these have a hole drilled in the center to accept the brass tubing inserted into the engines.

Early B-25s had a single collector exhaust pipe on the side of the nacelle. Late models had individual pipes exiting from fairings all around the cowl. I wanted to model an intermediate style of individual pipes exiting in groups behind the cowl flaps.

I made the exhaust pipes from a machined ring of PVC pipe. I cut slots in the ring with a jeweler's saw, then separated each into four sections: two each of four pipes and three pipes (**C**).

My next challenge was mating my new round cowlings to the slightly oval Monogram nacelles. I removed the fronts of the nacelles back to the prominent panel line and replaced them with sections of turned acrylic rod (**D**). I sanded the interface to blend the nacelles with the cowls.

A smaller rod with a hole drilled in it serves as the engine mount. This system allows the cowls to realistically stand out from the nacelles. The drilled hole accepts the brass tube from the engine.

The last chore was to cut the carburetor intakes from the Monogram cowl flap assemblies, clean them, and attach them to the cowls (**E**).

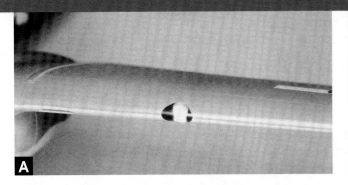

Small Details. I made the landing lights in the wing leading edges from aluminum turnings press-fit into small blocks of clear acrylic (A). After cementing the blocks into the wing, I sanded them to match the leading edge and polished them smooth.

I attached brass tubes to the rear of the propellers to fit inside the slightly larger tubes in the engines. I added sectioned brass tubes over the turbo outlets on top of the starboard wing (B).

I modified the gun packs from the Revell kit by thinning them down and adding an extra blister (C). I made new barrels from .040" brass wire and placed the top ones slightly forward of the bottom pair. The new

astro-compass blister was turned from acrylic.

After masking all clear panels I sprayed the model with lacquer primer. I removed the masks and sanded everything again, polished the clear panels, and masked them for the final time.

I did not attempt to replicate one specific aircraft, but I wanted the model to represent a typical B-25D strafer of the 501st Bomb Squadron, 345th Bomb Group, in May 1944. I first painted white stripes on the tail fins and orange on the cowl fronts, then masked these and applied a typical Olive Drab and Neutral Gray camouflage scheme. When the paint was dry, I scribed in panel lines and

applied decals. The nose art came from Monogram's P-61 and is only there because I like Snuffy Smith.

There it is: A detailed 1/48 scale desk model of the U.S. Army Air Force's most famous medium bomber!

CHAPTER THREE

World War II model paint guide

Seemingly defying gravity, Paul Boyer's Mitchell shows off more than just detail. Brass tubes mounted on the propeller and inside the engines allow the props to spin with just a little breeze.

World War II model paints used to be difficult to find. With the arrival of many new kits of WWII aircraft and armor, new paint colors have emerged from established paint companies.

By Paul Boyer

To make your search for the right military shade easier, we've listed the most common WWII colors in the accompanying table. The colors of the major powers are arranged by country along the left side of the table. Read across the table for paint brands. The manufacturer's stock numbers appear where the columns and rows intersect. We did not include black, white, or silver (aluminum) in this chart.

The chart provides you with an overall view of the paints available, but not their accuracy. Determine for yourself which paint you prefer.

COLOR	Gunze	Humbrol	Polly Scale	Tamiya	Testor	Testor Acryl	Xtracolor Enamel
UNITED STATES							
Navy light gray 602	H51	129	505090	-	1730	4763	X137
Neutral (sea) gray 603	H53	-	505086	XF53	1725	-	X133
Insignia blue 605	H326	-	-	-	1719	4742	X122
Non-spec. sea blue 607	H54	-	505092	XF17	1718	-	X121
Intermediate blue 608	H56	144	505094	XF18	1720	4744	X125
Azure blue 609	-	-	505262	-	2048	-	X26
Sky 610	H74	23	505254	XF21	2049	4840	X7
Interior green 611	H58	-	505096	XF4	1715	4852	X117
Yellow zinc chromate	-	-	-	-	1184	4851	-
Medium green 612	H303	117	505082	-	1713	-	X114
Olive drab 613	H52	155	505080	XF62	1711	4842	X112
Faded olive drab	-	-	505218	-	2051	-	X113
Orange yellow 614	H329	154	505220	XF3	1708	4721	X106
Middlestone 615	H71	84	505260	-	2052	-	X9
Sand 616	-	-	505084	-	2053	-	X105
Dark earth 617	H72	29	505252	XF64	2054	4846	X2
Bright red 619	H327	153	505020	-	1705	-	X103
Dark gull gray 621	H317	140	505378	-	1740	4755	X131
Glossy sea blue 623	H55	-	-	-	1717	4686	X121
Navy blue gray	H42	-	505088	-	2055	4847	X162
UNITED KINGDOM							
Sky ("Type S")	H74	23	505254	XF21	2049	4840	X7
Extra dark sea grey	H333	27	505264	-	1723	-	X5
Dark slate grey	-	102	505266	-	2056	-	X25
Ocean grey	-	106	505256	-	2057	-	X6
Medium sea grey	H335	165	505258	XF20	2058	-	X3
Dark sea grey	H75	164	-	-	2059	-	X4
Light slate grey	-	31	-	-	1793	-	X118
Dark green	H73	30	505250	XF61	2060	4849	X1
Dark earth	H72	29	505252	XF64	2054	4846	X2
Middlestone	H71	84	505260	-	2052	-	X9
Azure blue	-	-	505262	-	2048	-	X26
P.R.U. blue	-	-	505268	-	2061	-	X8
Interior grey-green	-	-	505270	-	2062	4850	X10
Trainer yellow	-	24	-	-	2063	-	X11
FRANCE							
Dark blue gray	-	65	505236	-	2105	-	-
Khaki	-	-	505238	-	2106	-	X384
Chestnut	-	98	505041	-	2107	-	-
Earth brown	-	-	505240	-	2108	-	-
Light blue gray	-	-	505242	-	2109	-	-
ITALY							
Sand	-	-	505284	-	2110	-	-
Dark brown	-	-	505286	-	2111	-	-
Dark olive green	-	102	505296	-	2112	-	-
Blue gray	-	64	505290	-	2113	-	-
Camouflage green	-	-	505288	-	-	-	-
Light blue gray 1	-	-	505242	-	-	-	-
Camouflage yellow 2	-	-	505292	-	-	-	-
Camouflage yellow 3	-	-	505294	-	-	-	-
GERMAN LUFTWAFFE							
Grau 02 (RLM gray)	H70	92	505075	XF22	2071	4770	X201
Gelb 04	-	-	505017	-	2072	4771	X213
Rot 23	-	-	505020	-	2073	4772	X217
Dunkelblau 24	-	-	505023	-	2074	4773	X218
Hellgrün 25	-	-	505026	-	-	4774	-
Dunkelbraun 61	-	-	505300	-	2075	4775	X219
Grün 62	-	-	505302	-	2076	4776	X220
Lichtgrau 63	-	-	505304	-	2077	4777	X221
Lichtblau 64	-	-	505306	-	-	-	-
Hellblau 65	H67	65	505051	-	2078	4778	X202
Schwarzgrau 66	-	-	505014	-	2079	4779	X203
Dark olive green 67	-	-	505308	-	-	-	-
Light olive green 68	-	-	505310	-	-	-	-
Light tan 69	-	-	505312	-	-	-	-

COLOR	Gunze	Humbrol	Polly Scale	Tamiya	Testor	Testor Acryl	Xtracolor Enamel
GERMAN LUFTWAFFE Continued							
Schwarzgrün 70	H65	91	505055	XF27	2080	4780	X204
Dunkelgrün 71	H64	30	505056	-	2081	4781	X205
Grün 72	-	-	505314	-	2082	4782	X222
Grün 73	-	-	505316	-	2083	4783	X223
Graugrün 74	H68	27	505059	-	2084	4784	X206
Grauviolett 75	H69	-	505060	-	2085	4785	X207
Lichtblau 76	-	-	505061	-	2086	4786	X208
Hellgrau 77	-	-	-	-	-	4787	-
Hellblau 78	-	-	505318	-	2087	4788	X214
Sandgelb 79	H66	62	505320	-	2088	4789	X209
Grün 80	-	-	505322	-	2089	4790	X215
Braunviolett 81	-	-	505070	-	2090	4791	X210
Dunkelgrün 82	-	-	505071	-	2091	4792	X211
Lichtgrün 83	-	-	505072	-	2092	4793	X212
Graublau 84	-	-	505324	-	-	4794	-
GERMAN ARMOR							
Panzer dark gray	-	-	505110	XF63	2094	4795	X800
Panzer dark yellow	H79	-	505111	XF60	2095	4796	X808
Panzer red brown	H47	-	505112	XF64	2096	4797	X807
Panzer olive green	-	-	505113	XF58	2097	4798	X806
Panzer interior buff	-	-	-	XF57	2104	4805	X818
Afrika Khakibraun '41	-	-	-	-	2098	-	X804
Afrika Grünbraun '41	-	-	-	-	2099	-	X803
Signalbraun	-	-	-	-	2100	-	X801
Anthracitgrau	-	-	-	-	2101	-	X802
Afrika Braun '42	-	-	-	-	2102	-	X808
Afrika Dunkelgrau '42	-	-	-	-	2103	-	X809
JAPAN							
Army green	H60	-	505272	XF13	2114	-	X351
Army light gray	H62	-	505274	XF14	2115	-	X352
Navy green	H59	-	505278	XF11	2116	-	X353
Navy sky gray	H61	-	505280	XF12	2117	-	X354
Deep yellow	-	-	505282	-	2118	-	-
Army brown	-	-	505276	-	-	-	-
Interior metallic blue	H63	-	-	X13	2119	-	X355
SOVIET UNION							
Marker red	-	174	-	-	2127	-	-
Marker yellow	-	99	-	-	2128	-	-
Light earth brown	-	-	505228	-	2124	-	-
Topside green	-	-	505230	-	2122	-	-
Underside blue	-	-	505226	-	2123	-	-
Dark topside gray	-	-	505232	-	2121	-	-
Light topside gray	-	-	505234	-	2120	-	-
Earth gray	-	-	-	-	2125	-	-
Topside blue	-	-	-	-	2126	-	-
Soviet armor green	-	-	-	-	2129	4807	-
AUSTRALIA							
177 Earth	-	-	505244	-	-	-	-
178 Foliage green	-	-	505246	-	-	-	-
195 Sky	-	-	505248	-	-	-	-

SOURCES
Gunze Sangyo Aqueous Hobby Color distributed by Marco Polo Import Inc., 532 S. Coralridge Place, City of Industry, CA 91746, 626-333-2328, www.marcopoloimport.com
Humbrol Marfleet, Hull, North Humberside HU9 5NE, England, 44-1428-701191
Polly Scale, Testor Model Master enamels, and Model Master Acryl Testor, 440 Blackhawk Park Ave., Rockford, IL 61104, 815-962-6654, www.testors.com
Tamiya Color distributed by Tamiya America, 2 Orion, Aliso Viejo, CA 92656-4200, 800-826-4922, www.tamiyausa.com
Xtracolor H.G. Hannant Ltd., Trafalgar House, 29-31 Trafalgar St., Lowestoft, Suffolk NR32 3AT, England, 44 1502 517444, www.hannants.co.uk

CHAPTER FOUR

Detailing Tamiya's Avro Lancaster

A CLASSIC MADE EVEN BETTER

Avro's Lancaster was the most famous British heavy bomber of World War II. Tamiya's kit is a beauty, but can be made even better with a little attention to detail.

Although Tamiya's 1/48 scale Lancaster was released in 1975, I finally got acquainted with it in 1994. A client wanted dropped flaps, an opened aft crew entry door (with interior detail added), and an opened pilot's side window—to better see a much-improved cockpit.

By Pat Hawkey

My reference for most of this detail work consisted mainly of four Lancaster cutaway drawings. They weren't definitive on everything and as a result, I employed artistic license here and there. My aim, though, was to make a convincing product.

Cockpit. Tamiya's cockpit is sparse, so I improved it. The instrument panel decal was used as a template for a new sandwiched sheet-styrene panel, **A**. The front "slice" was .010" sheet drilled out and instrument decals were placed on the rear slice to show through the holes. I simulated the raised engine boost and speed indicators with slices of rod stock. A small rectangular flying instrument panel was made from .010" sheet.

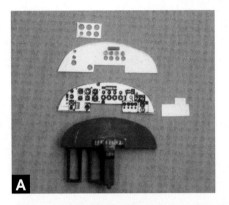

Tamiya provides only three bumps to represent throttle levers. I replaced them with four photoetched throttle levers from my spares. I also added bars across the rudder pedal frames, then painted everything flat black and dry-brushed silver, **B**.

The rest of the cockpit went together as supplied, except for the flight engineer's fold-down seat which I shortened by about half. I made seat belts with strips of lead foil. To make them look more realistic, I crumpled the strips between my fingertips, then carefully un-crumpled them, painted them khaki, and glued them to the seats. The navigator's swivel lamp was made from scratch and the railing at the bombardier's station was bent from Evergreen rod, **C**.

The oxygen hose is a Waldron Products item and the trim controls

pedestal on the pilot's right were cobbled together from spare parts. As in the rear fuselage, I sprinkled interior items to fill empty spaces.

At an early point in their service Lancaster cockpit interiors went from gray-green to black, so I painted mine a dark gray and again dusted the crevasses with black chalk pastel and dry-brushed everything with silver.

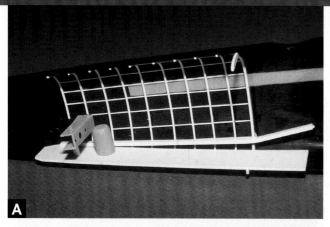

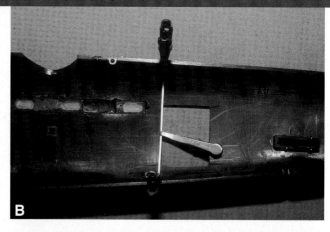

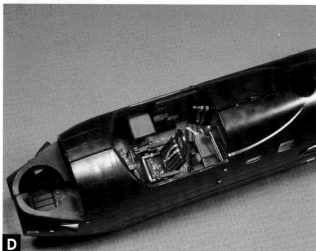

Fuselage interior. I glued in all the strips of clear oval windows. Most had sink marks in their centers, but the airplane I was modeling had these windows painted over, so I puttied and sanded them smooth. I also puttied and sanded the window strip on the inside opposite the right rear entry door. I didn't bother trying to represent painted-over windows on the inside.

I cut out the rear door by repeatedly scoring along the recessed outline until it came free. A new, thinner door was fashioned from .020" sheet styrene. This door opened in and to the right, which would help block the view forward, but there was still a lot of left-side fuselage interior to represent. Using the kit's external rivet pattern as a guide, I built up the internal structure with Evergreen strip styrene, **A.** I installed the ribs (vertical) first, then the stringers (horizontal) cut to fit between the ribs.

On the actual aircraft there was a main assembly break just aft of the upper turret and that's where I stopped the interior detail. I represented that major rib with thicker, wider sheet styrene. Looking aft, I installed a long, narrow box found in my spare-parts collection for the horizontal stabilizer spar.

The Elsan chemical toilet parked just forward of the spar was reshaped from a suitably sized bomb also from the parts box. Ammo troughs leading to the rear turret were more sections of Evergreen strip, and though none of my references could prove there was a proper floor back there, I put one in to make it look better.

In the right fuselage half I framed the door opening with more strip, **B,** and added a step immediately inside the doorway. I painted everything that would be seen RAF interior gray-green (maybe it should've been night black like the rest of the inte-

rior, but the green is more interesting). I added an assortment of boxes and interior shapes from various Monogram bomber kits to make things look busy. Finally I brushed dark-gray chalk pastels into all the corners and around the equipment to add depth, then lightly dry-brushed silver over everything to add highlights, **C.**

There are six small windows up front that were not overpainted, so I polished the clear kit parts and carefully glued them in place. After I was satisfied with the internal arrangement, I glued the fuselage halves together, **D.** Everything that can be seen looks nicely cramped.

Two emergency exits in the top of the fuselage contain round windows. Tamiya provides clear rectangular panels (that don't fit well) with the outline of the window molded in. Since there would be nothing to see inside, I painted their inside

E

F

faces black and glued them in place.

Tamiya didn't mold the three recognition lamps under the rear fuselage. (The rear quarter of the H2S blister, if carried, remained clear so they could be seen.) While they are shown in numerous references, none mentions their colors. I drilled them in and decided to paint one red, one yellow, and one green.

Tamiya turrets can be built separately and installed after the fuselage is sealed. The turrets don't have much detail, so I added some and made a few corrections. I added major braces

and sights from strip styrene and made ammo belts from lead foil folded in layers to the correct thickness, **E**.

The downward stagger of the rear turret inboard guns needed to be increased, and exterior shell-ejection troughs were added from Evergreen sheet styrene.

There's not enough clearance for the gun mounts inside the nose turret, so the barrels don't extend far enough out of the turret. I made the necessary adjustments.

The top turret clear parts are

molded in upper and lower halves (the only way Tamiya could capture the bulged shape) and the fit is not great when they are oh so carefully glued together. Fortunately the seam is a frame line. I like the way the finished top turret drops perfectly into place, **F**. It's easily removed to provide a finger hole to handle the model.

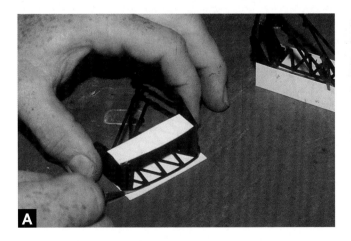

A

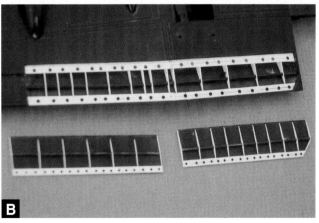

B

Wings and cowls. The first step here is to build the intricate, 15-piece main gear assemblies. I suggest cementing only enough of the bracing struts to allow you to pry apart the main struts so you can pop the wheels in after the model is finished. I used True Details bulged resin tires

on this model. I also added .010" sheet walls to the outer sides to blank off the wing interiors, **A**.

If you intend to drop the flaps, cut them out of the bottom wing halves and carefully glue the wings together, incorporating the finished undercarriage assemblies as spacing guides for

the gap between the wing halves at the flap line. Work the inboard engine nacelles into this operation as well.

There's a fair amount of interior flap and wing structure showing when Lancaster flaps are lowered. I followed the cutaway drawings and the exterior rivet patterns as I added

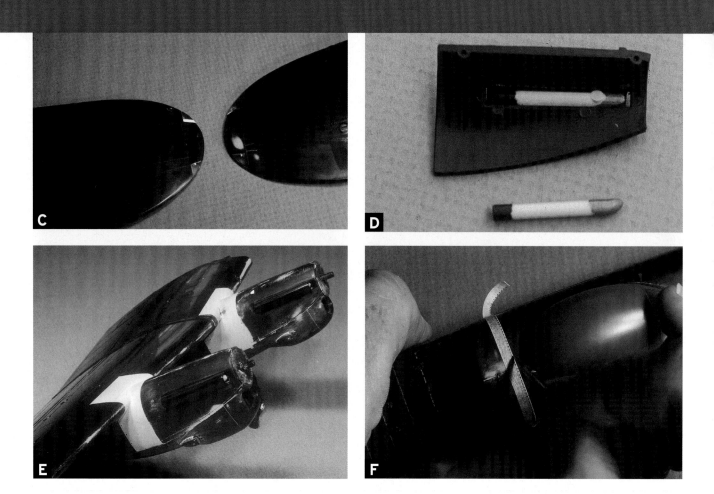

.015" styrene strip ribs and formers to the inside of the top wing surface and flaps, **B**. Between the ribs, went measured styrene rod. Last were the bordering strips with their 40 (per side) lightening holes.

The rear sections of the inner engine nacelles slid into the main nacelles when the flaps came down, so I cut them off at the break line and carved and sanded them to fit.

For some reason the kit's wing-tip navigation and formation lights weren't the same sizes, and none of them fit well. I could not imagine why the left and right lights wouldn't be the same size, so I made them the same on the model. I drilled a small hole into the leading-edge clear parts and filled them with red (left) and green (right) paint to indicate the enclosed lamp, **C**. The trailing-edge lenses (formation lights) housed three lamps—I guessed red, white, and green.

I replaced the kit's faint radiator screens with fine wire mesh, then painted the clear "fly screens" in front of the carburetor intakes black and lightly dry-brushed with silver.

The biggest fit challenge in the kit was the engine nacelles. Tamiya provides two basic Merlin power plants which can be exposed by leaving off cowl sections. There aren't enough exhaust stacks to go around if you leave out the engines and close the cowls, so I made new ones from sprue, **D**. These fit into the dampers in the cowl panels.

I had to use lots of gap-filling super glue and sandpaper to get the nacelles to fit the wings, **E**. The radiator shutters on the bottoms of the cowls were redefined with a scribing tool, but would look even better if replaced with new ones made from sheet styrene.

The surface detail of this kit is superb, but it is all raised rivets. Anything less than a perfect fit means sanding, and that means good-bye rivets. To replace the multitude I had sanded away, I measured the distance between rivets on the wings and made hash marks on a thin strip of masking tape. I used this as a guide to impress new rivets into the plastic with a scribing tool, **F**. You have to look close to see the difference between the raised originals and the new recessed rivets.

The wings and stabilizers join the fuselage without problems. The canopy fits well, too. I carefully sawed and filed away the pilot's sliding window and replaced it with .015" clear sheet. The real challenge here was to glue it securely in place and have no glue show. I used a white glue called Z RC-56 (found in the flying-model section of hobby shops). It dries glossy clear and gives a strong yet elastic bond.

REFERENCES
Avro Lancaster Bill Sweetman, Zokeisha Publications Ltd., New York, 1982
Avro Lancaster: Famous Airplanes of the World No. 88, Bunrin-Do, August 1977
Bombers of World War II Vol. 1 Squadron/Signal Publications, Carrollton, Texas, 1981
Guns in the Sky Chaz Boyer, Charles Scribner's Sons, New York, 1979
History of the RAF Chaz Boyer, Crescent Books, New York, 1977
Scale Models "Lancaster," August 1975
Lancaster in Action R.S.G. Mackay, Squadron/Signal Publications, Carrollton, Texas, 1982
Royal Air Force Yearbook 1976 *"Liturgy for the Lancaster,"* Neil Williams, Ducimus Books Ltd., London,1976

SOURCES
Sheet, tube, and rod styrene Evergreen Scale Models, 12808 NE 125th Way, Kirkland, WA 98034
True Details wheels Squadron Mail Order, 1115 Crowley Drive, Carrollton, TX 75011-5010, 214-242-8663
Instrument panels Waldron Model Products, P.O. Box 431, Merlin, OR 97532 503-474-1159

Finish. I sprayed the fins white and then yellow for the tail bands. When the paint was dry, I masked the bands and painted the rest of the model. I used a little white mixed with Testor Model Master gloss black for the undersurface and fin color. After carefully masking the long, straight fuselage demarcation line, I airbrushed Xtracolor gloss dark earth and dark green camouflage.

I used the kit decals, but the roundels and fin flashes were printed on separate sheets and used different reds. I ended up mixing my own shade of British brick red, airbrushed it on to red SuperScale decal stock, and cut my own roundel centers and fin flashes. (Actually, the wing roundels were totally new, cut with a compass and blade as the kit decals were too small.) I carefully trimmed all the clear film from the Tamiya code letters and sprayed them with my red mix so everything matched.

The kit decals snuggled to the gloss finish nicely. When they were dry, I sprayed the entire model with Testor Dullcote thinned 1:1 with Floquil Dio-Sol.

Photos reveal that most active Lancs were heavily weathered, but since my model carried no mission markers, I made it a fresh machine. I lightly painted exhaust streaks, and added minimal oil and dirt streaks with dark pastels. The antenna wires are stretched sprue.

I poured about 150 hours of work into the big Lancaster. The customer was happy, so what else could I ask for? How about a 1/48 scale injection-molded Halifax?

CHAPTER FIVE

Modeling a Midway hero's plane

IMPROVEMENTS FOR MONOGRAM'S TBD-1 DEVASTATOR

This TBD-1 carries on a grand tradition of World War II aircraft produced by Monogram—but the Devastator wreaks more havoc with a few well-placed details and some aftermarket accessories.

Nearly 60 years ago—June 1942—American airmen defeated the Japanese fleet at Midway. It was a move that thwarted Japan's conquest of the Pacific Ocean in World War II. Of all the heroes in this desperate struggle, one of the best known is U.S. Navy torpedo-bomber pilot George Gay. He flew in the first wave of planes attacking the Japanese Imperial Fleet— and was the only one of his group to survive.

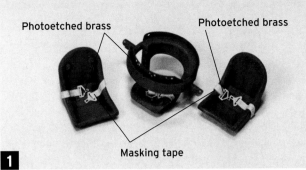

Photoetched brass

Photoetched brass

Masking tape

1 Photoetched brass and masking tape merge in the seat details.

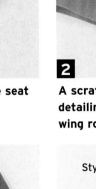

Scratchbuilt controls

Strip styrene

2 A scratchbuilt throttle quadrant revs up the interior detailing. Outside, strip styrene fills the gap at the wing root.

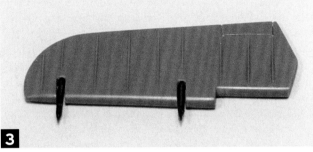

3 Hinge-pin inserts make dropped elevators look more realistic.

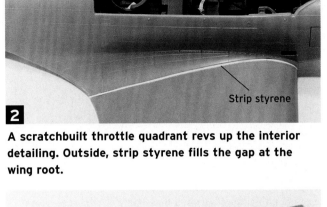

Styrene strips

4 Details sanded off the flaps were replaced with styrene strips.

By Phillip Gore

Searching for a kit to model the intrepid Gay's aircraft, I found Monogram's TBD-1, first produced in 1974. This model was part of Monogram's second generation of 1/48 scale kits, following those made in the late 1950s.

The kit is generally good in detail and accurate in shape. I figured it was perfect for adding my own touches without getting bogged down in a major project.

Open-canopy policy. I decided on an open canopy for my TBD in order to reveal extra details. I equipped all three seats with belts made from masking tape. Then I added buckles and harnesses from Tom's Model-works' photoetched brass detail set for WWII Navy aircraft (No. 208). The rear gunner's station received a photoetched brass bracing ring, **1**.

A scratchbuilt throttle quadrant is mounted on the port side for the pilot, **2**. I drilled holes in the consoles on either side, attached stretched-sprue levers with glue, and angled the kit's joystick back a little. To represent electrical wiring, I glued fine wires along the fuselage walls.

Aft and fore on the fuselage. I cut the rudder from the fuselage and notched out the rudder hinge. After drilling a hole in the center of the notch I inserted a $1/16$" rod as a hinge pin. A corresponding hole drilled in the upper fin of the fuselage accepted this pin when the rudder was installed. This procedure was repeated on the stabilizers/elevators, **3**, but I angled the hinge pins because the elevators would be dropped.

On the cowling, I bored out the gunport and carefully sawed the cowl flaps to separate them. The bombardier deck serves as a false floor above the torpedo mount to block the view into what would otherwise be a hollow-looking fuselage.

Wings and things. I glued together the wing halves, aligning them at the corrugated notches on the wings' leading edges. Sanding this area required care to ensure the corru-

gated sections remained uniform.

With the landing gear down, open areas underneath the wings invited further details. I turned the plane upside down, added various bits and pieces of styrene and wiring to the upper inboard wing parts, and glued everything with super glue and five-minute epoxy. I laid a straightedge over the entire wing to make sure the tips weren't drooping.

After the glue had dried, I test-fitted the wings to the fuselage. Large gaps at the roots were spliced with styrene strip. When I was satisfied with the fit I glued the wings in place.

I modeled the wing flaps in a dropped position, detailing recessed areas and the inside of the kit flaps with bracing made from strips of styrene, **4**.

Sanding and smoothing seams and joints also erased some raised panel lines, **5**. To restore the lines, I cut narrow, straight-edged masking tape pieces and carefully placed them on either side of an original panel line. I airbrushed between the

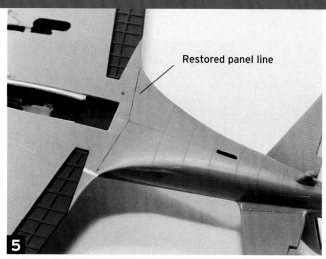

Restored panel line

5

Excess paint is not always bad—here it replaces panel lines lost during sanding.

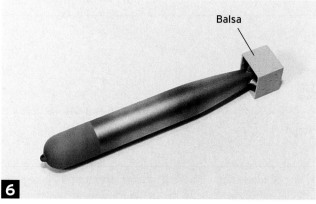

Balsa

6

Adding a balsa stabilizer fin to the torpedo keeps the modeling on target.

Early war Navy colors and markings

U.S. Navy aircraft color schemes changed rapidly as the United States prepared for war. In 1939, when World War II began in Europe, Navy carrier aircraft were painted in brilliant aluminum with chrome yellow wings. Bright tail colors coded each airplane to its carrier. An order, dated Dec. 30, 1940, required an overall paint scheme of light gray for carrier aircraft. On Aug. 20, 1941, another order added blue gray to all surfaces seen from above (this included the bottom surfaces of folded wings on some aircraft, the Devastator among them).

The TBD flown by Ensign George Gay at Midway was a well-traveled aircraft (Bureau No. 1518) that had been ordered by the U.S. Navy in August 1938. The plane had flown with a few Marine units plus Navy torpedo squadrons VT-3 and VT-6 before being assigned to the Navy's VT-8 in April 1942. The wings and fuselage of Gay's Devastator carried "medium-size" national insignias, replacing the larger insignias called for in early 1942. The markings were still fairly new at the Battle of Midway, so they were relatively bright and unfaded.

The markings on the fuselage side ("T-14") were incomplete. The code should have been "8-T-14," indicating the fourteenth aircraft of Torpedo Eight, the torpedo aircraft squadron assigned to the eighth carrier, the USS Hornet. The incomplete code could have been a result of the aircraft's recent transfer. Also, it could have been designed to disguise the aircraft's origin because of the possibility of it falling into Japanese hands.

– Paul Boyer

tape with several coats of primer until the paint built up to the height of the original panel line. After each new panel line had dried, I gently buffed it with a soft cloth to smooth and slightly round it. I added engine ignition wires, an oil line from the crankcase, and an ignition ring. A small box of balsa wood represents an aerodynamic stabilizer assembly on the torpedo, **6**. I replaced support struts on the kit's landing gear with styrene rods bent to more accurate shapes, and installed small sections of insulated electrical wire to replicate brake lines.

Painting. After masking off the plane's interior, I temporarily attached the engine and cowling with white glue and coated the lower surfaces of the aircraft with Testor Model Master Light Gray (No. 2038). Airbrushing this with a wash of

darker gray simulated wear on various underside panels.

Next, I masked the light gray areas and airbrushed the upper parts and the bottoms of the outboard wing sections with Model Master U.S. Navy Blue Gray (No. 2055). I weathered the base coat by over-spraying the wings, stabilizers, and upper fuselage with a thin coat of the base color mixed with a few drops of white, **7**.

After more masking, I airbrushed walkways on the wings black, followed by a light wash of light gray, and I penciled in rear-gun storage doors on the fuselage, **8**.

After everything dried I airbrushed the entire plane and any loose parts with a heavy clear coat of Future and applied the decals (from various Superscale and Yellowhammer sheets), sealing them with another coat of Future. Coating the model

with a 50-50 mix of Testor Dullcote (No. 1160) and Model Master Metalizer Thinner (No. 1419) gave it a uniform finish.

A few final details. I got a twin-mount .30-caliber machine gun from a Hasegawa SBD-3 kit (No. 09119) and improved it with photoetched brass parts from Tom's Modelworks, **8**, then glued the finished loose parts in place. Most of the details were in place before the canopy was attached, **9**.

I covered the kit canopy frames with an E-Z Mask vinyl masking set (No. 108), then painted the frames and attached the canopy with white glue (not styrene glue or super glue, either of which would fog the clear parts).

I added a pitot tube, modifying it by cutting off its end and installing three pieces of wire bent to shape. Also, I cut a tiny piece of brass mesh to fit the oil-cooler inlet. For various

7

A light overspray bleaches the base color for a sun-baked appearance.

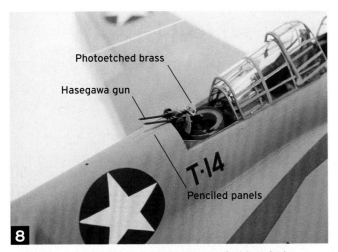

8

Photoetched brass

Hasegawa gun

T-14

Penciled panels

A Hasegawa machine gun is accompanied by photo-etched brass details and panel lines drawn with pencil.

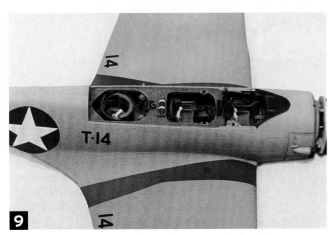

9

T-14

With its interior details nearly done, the aircraft stands ready to receive a canopy.

George Gay—sole survivor

At their launch from the USS Hornet on June 4th, 1942, George Gay and many other Torpedo Eight squadron pilots were ensigns, fresh from pilot training or stateside duty. Gay had never flown off a carrier with a torpedo before; in fact, he had never even seen it done! Nevertheless, his TBD-1 Devastator and 14 others took off and pursued the Japanese fleet in a battle that changed the tide of the Pacific war.

Before Torpedo Eight's planes could reach the Japanese carriers, many were cut down one-by-one by Zeros. Of the 15 TBDs, only Gay's reached the fleet. By the time he hurled his torpedo against a carrier, he was wounded and his rear gunner killed. After dropping his "fish," Gay flew his crippled plane over his target, enduring heavy gunfire. Zeros joined the attack and shot him down.

He escaped his sinking plane and clung to floating debris as the battle exploded all around him. Gay was found the next day by a Navy PBY Catalina crew and sent home to recuperate. He then served with Torpedo Eleven during the Guadalcanal campaign. After the war, Gay flew 30 years as a TWA pilot.

George Gay was one of the more accessible heroes of the war and was a popular speaker and guest at many veterans' and modelers' conventions. After his death in 1994, his ashes were scattered at the Midway battle site, there to rejoin his squadron mates of Torpedo Eight.

– Paul Boyer

REFERENCES
A Glorious Page in Our History R. Cressman, S. Ewing, B. Tillman, M. Horan, C. Reynolds, S. Coen, Pictorial Histories Publishing Co., Missoula, MT, 1990
TBD-1 Devastator in Action Al Adcock, Squadron Signal Publications, Carrollton, Texas, 1989
U.S. Aircraft Carriers in Action Part 1 Robert Stern, Squadron Signal Publications, Carrollton, Texas, 1991

SOURCES
Photoetched detail parts Tom's Modelworks, 1050 Cranberry Dr., Cupertino, CA 95014, 408-777-8667, www.tomsmodelworks.com
Styrene components Evergreen Scale Models, 18620-F 141st Ave. NE, Woodinville, WA 98072, 877-376-9099
Masks E-Z Masks, RR 4, Smith Falls, ON, Canada K7A4S5
Decals Superscale International, 2360 Apache Dr., Bishop, CA 93514, www.superscale.com
Yellowhammer distributed by Meteor Productions, P.O. Box 3956, Merrifield, VA 22116-3956, 703-971-0500, www.meteorprod.com
Kristal-Kleer Microscale Industries, 18435 Bandilier Circle, Fountain Valley, CA 92708

identification and formation lights on the wings, fuselage, rudder, and left front stabilizer, I used Kristal-Kleer or drops of five-minute epoxy. The final touch was an antenna made from a fine-filament fishing line.

This project might sound like a lot of work at first, but most of these details were easy to add—and, as always in modeling, the details make the difference. Modeling Gay's plane was a tribute to the bravery and resolve that produced an American victory in the decisive Battle of Midway.

CHAPTER SIX

Detailing Revell's 1/32 Scale P-47 Thunderbolt

A CLASSIC "RAZORBACK JUG" OF WWII ACE FRANCIS GABRESKI

As big as they get. The massive P-47 Thunderbolt model by Revell receives Paul Budzik's superdetailing treatment. Scratchbuilt landing gear and an intricately detailed engine are among his improvements. Paul Budzik photos.

No matter how you look at it, Republic's P-47 Thunderbolt is an impressive airplane. Its large size makes it an equally impressive replica in 1/32 scale, but the old Revell kit's inaccuracies have kept enthusiasts from seeing its real value: a palette for the detailer's brush.

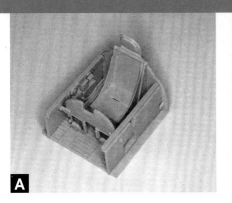

A

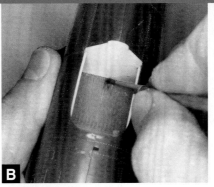

B

C

D

E

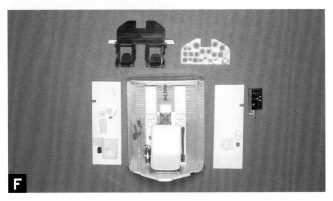

F

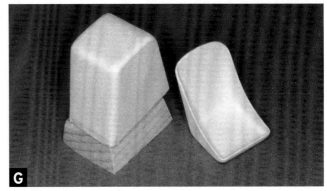

G

By Paul Budzik

I started this project by comparing the features of the real aircraft with the kit, then decided what modifications would capture the features of the prototype. After looking through my references, I found that most P-47s were parked with cowl flaps open and wing flaps up (despite a training film's suggestions to the contrary). The elevators were frequently dropped several degrees. Most often the tires had a diamond tread pattern. I wanted to incorporate these features in my model, along with improvements to the landing gear, engine, and cockpit.

Cockpit Improvements. The stock cockpit is spartan even for a kit of this vintage (**A**). I made a new cockpit floor from two pieces of acrylic sheet, then carved ribs into it with a grinding bit in a miniature milling machine. Using the kit's rear bulkhead as a guide, I cut a new one from .030" styrene. I traced the outline of the front of the razorback onto the bulkhead, then cut it to fit inside the taped together fuselage. Next, I cemented the new front and rear bulkheads to the floor (**B**).

I cut new cockpit walls from .030" sheet styrene using the kit walls as a guide for the height (**C**).

With thin strips of styrene cemented to the front and rear bulk-

heads to hold the walls in position, I built the remaining tub structure with sheet acrylic and styrene (**D**).

I sanded the kit instrument panel/rudder pedal assembly thin and used it as a mount for new scratchbuilt items. I photoetched my own instrument panel (**E**) and used a reduced photo image of an instrument panel for the gauges (see "Photoetching for modelers," July 1991 FSM). I cut notches in the sidewalls to locate the panel and pedal assembly, then fashioned troughs for the rudder pedals from sheet styrene and cemented them to the floor (**F**). I vacuum-formed a new seat over a homebuilt form (**G**), and built the supporting frame from brass wire and machinings.

H

I

All the boxes in the cockpit were milled from acrylic rod, while the control stick, manual hydraulic pump, and flap equalizer were machined from brass. I used brass wire and machinings for the buttons and knobs along with some of Waldron's P-47 placards.

I made the oxygen hose by wrapping .015" solder around another piece of wire. The hose and regulator were fit onto the fuselage before the tub was in place. I added the throttle quadrant after painting so it wouldn't be in the way.

The finished cockpit looks a lot better than the one provided in the kit (**H** and **I**).

Fuselage. I wanted to pose the cowl flaps open, so I needed to cut the cowling from the fuselage halves. First, I cemented and filled the seams around the cowling panels, then carefully scored around the edge of the cowl from the inside with multiple passes of a hobby knife. I wanted to cut almost all the way through, so it would be easy to snap apart later on. Next, I held the fuselage halves together with rubber bands and applied cement to glue only the cowl portions together. Once set, I carefully snapped the cowling from the fuselage; this left me with a small lip to help me relocate the cowling later.

I replaced Revell's flat intercooler ramps in the aft fuselage sides with curved ramps I produced by vacuum forming over a wood mold (**A**). I boxed them in with sheet styrene. I added the intercooler doors just before painting to keep them out of the way while I sanded and rescribed the fuselage. I improved the other vents and doors on the bottom rear fuselage, then glued the fuselage

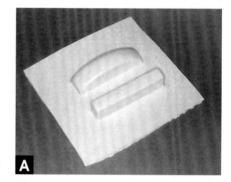

A

halves together, incorporating the cockpit tub and engine fire wall.

Engine detail. One of the things I like about radial engines is that I can superdetail the power plant without opening panels that destroy the lines of the airplane. I assembled the cylinder banks as per the instructions but spent time removing the molded ignition wires. I drilled holes in the cylinders to accept new ignition wires, then removed a little plastic from the back of the front cylinder row to place the two rows closer together. After gluing the cylinder banks together, I placed the engine in the lathe and bored a hole through

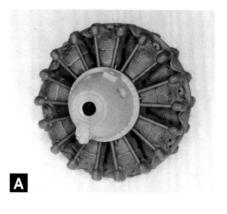

A

the center to accept a ⁵⁄₃₂" brass tube long enough to anchor in the fire wall and extend past the gear case.

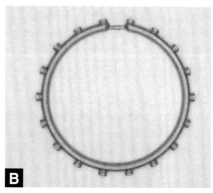

B

Revell's gear case didn't look right, so I made a new one that looked more authentic. First, I cut a hole in

30

C

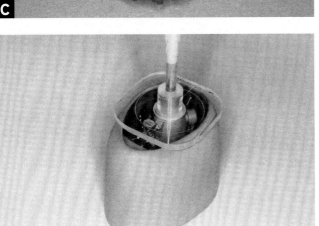

D

SOURCE
Photoetched detail parts: Waldron Model Products, P.O. Box 431, Merlin, OR 97532

REFERENCES
Republic P-47 Thunderbolt Aero Publishers staff, Aero Publishers, Inc., Fallbrook, California, 1966
P-47 Thunderbolt in Action (No. 67) Larry Davis, Squadron/Signal Publications, Inc., Carrollton, Texas, 1984
Camouflage & Markings, Republic P-47 Thunderbolt, U.S.A.A.F., E.T.O. & M.T.O., 1942-45 Roger A. Freeman, Ducimus Books Limited, London, England
The Mighty Eighth, A History of the US 8th Army Air Force Roger A. Freeman, Doubleday and Company, Inc., Garden City, New York, 1970
Republic Thunderbolt Freeman, Roger A., Ducimus Books Ltd., London
Thunderbolt, A Documentary History of the Republic P-47 Roger A. Freeman, Charles Scribner & Sons, New York, 1978
U.S. Army Air Force Fighters, Part Two William Green and Gordon Swanborough, Arco Publishing Company, Inc., New York, 1978
P-47 Thunderbolt at War William N. Hess, Doubleday and Company, Inc., Garden City, New York, 1976
The P-47 Thunderbolt Len Morgan, Arco Publishing Co., New York, 1963
USAAF Fighters of World War Two, In Action Michael O'Leary, Blandford Press, Dorset, England, 1986
Aerodata International No. 6, Republic P-47D Thunderbolt John B. Rabbets, Visual Art Productions Ltd., Oxford, England, 1978
Republic P-47D Thunderbolt, Aircraft Profile No. 7 Edward Shacklady, Profile Books Limited, Berkshire, England, 1981
Aces of the Eighth Gene B. Stafford and William N. Hess, Squadron/Signal Publications, Carrollton, Texas,1973
Thunderbolt in Action (No. 18) Gene B. Stafford, Squadron/Signal Publications, Inc., Warren, Michigan,1975
P- 7 Thunderbolt Reprints of Pilots Manual, Aviation Publications, Appleton, Wisconsin, 1978

E

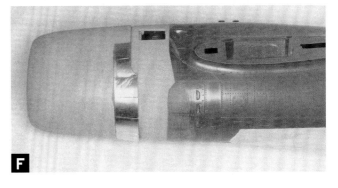

F

piece of sheet styrene, then cemented it in place over the front of the cylinder banks. I drilled holes to accept bits of .028" steel wire which simulate the nuts and bolts on the base of the gear case. Next, I turned a new gear from acrylic rod, then added the oil drain, magneto mount, and holes for the distributors. After cementing the gear case in place (**A**), I added .032" wire pushrods into holes drilled around the circumference of the crankcase.

Next came the wiring harness, which I made by machining a brass ring, then press fitting tiny brass machinings into holes drilled around the ring (**B**). I mounted the ring with .016" wire supports that fit into

holes drilled into the engine behind the gear case.

I had to paint and assemble in stages to create a realistic look to the engine. First, I airbrushed the cylinders Floquil Grimy Black, the gear case gray, and the wiring harness flat aluminum. Next I brushed the pushrods with Testor gloss black, then inserted sections of hypodermic needle to simulate spark plugs on the cylinders. At this stage I could epoxy the wiring harness in place, add the acrylic rod distributors, and repaint the gear case. I added unpainted copper wire for the spark plug wires to simulate the shielding. Finally, I machined brass for the prop governor and magneto (**C**).

With that big open front end, I wanted to be sure the engine was properly aligned in the cowling, so I made an alignment jig. I scribed a circle in a scrap of sheet acrylic, then drilled a hole in the circle's center. The brass tubing that fits through the engine also fits through this hole while the acrylic sheet rests against the front of the cowl (**D**). I anchored the engine to the cowl by applying small dabs of dental acrylic between the cylinder heads and the inside of the cowl. Dental acrylic contains a solvent that reacts with styrene, so the material bonds to the plastic when set.

To help anchor the engine/cowl subassembly to the fuselage, I drilled

G

H

an oversize hole in the kit's engine mount, larger than a piece of telescoping brass tubing I placed over the tube projecting from the back of the engine. I applied a little dental resin to the outside of this new tube, and positioned the cowling on the fuselage. When set, the resin fills the space in the oversize hole. Now I could slide the engine/cowl off the fuselage while the outside tube remains in the engine mount. I repeated this telescoping tubing technique on the bottom of the engine to ensure correct alignment (E).

Next, I evened off the front of the fuselage with .080" styrene to represent the rounded structure under the cowl flaps. I marked the location of the cowl flaps, then removed the plastic, leaving a shallow lip to serve as a mount for my new cowl flaps. I cut the flaps from .005" shim brass and formed them to the contour of the cowl (F). To position them properly, I placed the cowl on the fuselage and built up a spacer with layers of masking tape. Now the flaps could lie in the shallow lip and rest on the tape spacer as I secured them to the cowl with super glue. Once this had set, I removed the cowl and took off the tape spacer.

I formed the forward intercooler doors and the oil cooler shutters (G) from .005" shim brass and cemented them with super glue. The rear turbo doors are also made from shim brass (H).

A

B

Wings, guns, and tail. The kit's main landing gear mounts are skimpy, so I replaced them with small blocks of acrylic. I added sprue inside the wing root to stiffen the wing structure.

After cementing the wing halves together, I cut out the navigation lights at the tips, replaced them with clear acrylic, and sanded and polished them to shape. I glued the wings to the fuselage, then drilled the mounting holes for the gear struts all the way through the top surface of the wing. I inserted short pieces of brass tubing which would eventually hold the main struts. According to reference photos, the struts canted outboard about three degrees at the wing, then bent perpendicular to the ground. The kit struts were incorrect, so I made new ones from brass tubing, wire, and machinings.

I machined and carved a new tire from acrylic, then used this as a pattern to make an RTV mold for polyester resin castings (A). I sanded the bottoms of the tires for a realistic appearance (B).

Revell molded the machine guns along the center line of the wing, but the real aircraft's weapons were aligned parallel with the ground. I cut away the kit guns, then bored oversize holes along the correct line in the leading edges. Next I made a jig from scrap acrylic. I drilled four $3/32$" holes at the proper interval with a drill press, then inserted four lengths of

$3/32$" brass tubing. The jig held the tubes in the proper alignment against the wing as I added dental acrylic resin into the oversize holes (C). Once the resin set, I removed the jig, cut off the tubes, and sanded them smooth with the leading edge. After the model was painted, I inserted $1/16$" tubing into the tubes in the wing to represent the gun barrels.

I cut the elevators free from the horizontal stabilizers then cleaned up

C

the edges to prepare them for reattachment (D). I wanted the elevators facing down slightly and mounted them to a short brass rod that runs

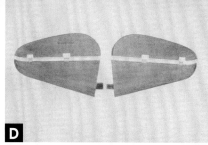

D

through a hole drilled in rudder. I refined the rudder trim tab control arm and the rear navigation light with brass rod and wire.

Drop tank, prop, and paint. I used a 108-gallon paper tank from a 1/32 scale Hasegawa P-51D. I glued the tank halves together, then sanded all the detail away. I masked the front and rear portions with artist's striping tape, then sprayed the tank with a lacquer primer. After sanding, I removed the tape, leaving a subtle simulation of the doped paper. I machined the upper attachment points from brass and acrylic stock. I airbrushed the tank with Floquil silver, then used adhesive metal foil for the circumferential bands (A). Styrene makes up the fuselage center line mount, while brass machinings and wire make up the sway braces.

I cut the blades from the kit propeller and built a new hub assembly from brass machinings. I machined the spinner from aluminum and painted the hub with a touch of Testor Chrome Silver and Floquil Reefer Grey. I like this combination of paints for a flat aluminum appearance. I cleaned the prop blades and adapted them to press fit into the hub assembly (B). Now I have a working variable-pitch prop!

I first applied white for the front of the cowl, code letters, and identification bands on the tail. After the white had thoroughly dried, I lightly sanded it to minimize the grainy texture.

Next, I masked the areas to remain white and applied the camouflage col-

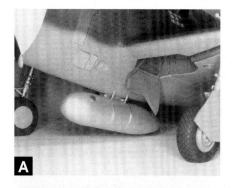

A

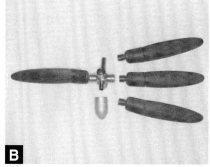

B

C

ors, Olive Drab and Neutral Gray. The decals were a mix of whatever I could find in the right size. The insignias in the kit were too large according to my references, so I replaced them with aftermarket items.

My model represents a Razorback T-Bolt that Maj. Francis Gabreski flew in late 1943. "Gabby" went on to become the top-scoring ace in the European theater, with 38 confirmed air-to-air victories. I made the victory symbols from layers of solid-color decal topped off with swastikas cut

out of Super Scale sheet. I started with a white rectangle, then applied a red rectangle, white circle, and the swastika (C). Finally, I air brushed the entire model with Testor Dullcote.

Whew! This model required a lot of work, and I could do more, but what an improvement over the kit as it comes from the box!

CHAPTER SEVEN

Alfonso Martinez Berlana's maritime Ju 188A in 1/48 Scale

THE SPANISH MASTER UPGRADES DRAGON'S LUFTWAFFE BOMBER

The combination of the brutally utilitarian look of the Ju 188 and the oddly banded camouflage makes this 1/48 scale model of a German anti-ship aircraft appealing.

Here at *FSM,* we always look forward to model photos from Spain's Alfonso

Martinez Berlana, and this spectacular Ju 188 is a real eye-popper! The

zebra-striped, bulbous-nosed Junkers stands out among the usual dark

colors in a Luftwaffe collection.

Eduard photoetched cockpit details

Verlinden machine guns

AeroMaster decals

ProModeler Ju 88
bombs and racks
(underneath)

True Details wheels

The winter banded camouflage was not applied to the fin and rudder.

**Photos by Aurelio Gimeno Ruiz
and Alfonso Martinez Berlana**

Alfonso's models are always spectacular to look at, and often he graces us with in-progress photos to show the work he put into the project.

The subject he chose this time was a Ju 188 bomber based in Norway to attack Allied shipping approaching the Soviet Union. He was intrigued by the striped camouflage; each plane was unique because there was no paint regulation. The overpainted light blue-gray stripes helped blend the bomber into the winter background.

Alfonso told us the 1/48 scale Dragon kit looked impressive in the box, but the fit and finish of the parts needed work. To build the bomber as it was equipped, Alfonso had to

Junkers Ju 188

Developed as a private venture from the successful Ju 88, the Ju 188 was rushed into service when the more advanced Ju 288 proved to be a failure. Designed to be powered by either BMW 801 or Junkers Jumo 213 engines, the Ju 188 carried a crew of four and could hoist as much as 6,615 pounds of bombs or torpedoes.

The first Ju 188E (BMW engines) entered service in May 1943. Many Ju 188A (Jumo engines) were completed as Ju 188D reconnaissance aircraft, and Ju 188F models were also reconnaissance craft with BMW engines. The production run of the Ju 188 was 1,076; a little more than half were D's or F's.

An interesting sidenote: After World War II, the French Aéronavale obtained at least 30 captured Ju 188s to use as land-based bombers!

– Paul Boyer

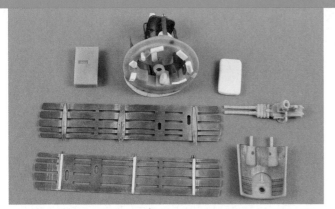

PROJECT AT A GLANCE
Dragon Ju 188 (kit No. 5517)
ProModeler Ju 88 (No. 5948 for bombs and racks)
Eduard photoetched-brass detail set (No. 48147)
True Details wheels (No. 48029)
Verlinden aircraft machine guns (No. 1261)
AeroMaster decals (No. 48-145)
Evergreen styrene sheet, strip, rod, and tube

Alfonso added detail to the dorsal gun turret, and used photoetched brass dive brakes under the wings. The resin machine guns are from Verlinden.

The right side of the painted cockpit shows the radio gear and a small bench seat with seat belts.

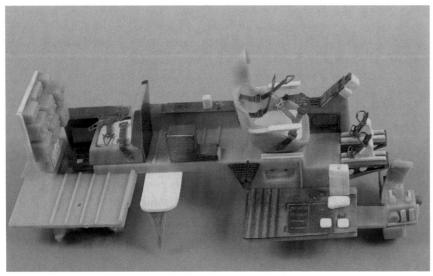

Eduard photoetched brass details are easy to pick out in this view of the unpainted cockpit tub. White parts are styrene stock.

cannibalize bombs and bomb racks from the ProModeler Ju 88 (which is another Dragon kit). Dragon's Ju 188 came with torpedoes which Alfonso chose not to use.

To improve the Dragon kit, Alfonso employed an Eduard photoetched brass detail set, True Details wheels, Verlinden aircraft machine guns, and an AeroMaster decal sheet.

The majority of the Eduard set is dedicated to the cockpit. Alfonso painted the interior with Vallejo acrylic RLM 66 Schwarzgrau and RLM 02 Grau. On the outside, Alfonso painted the underside light blue RLM 65 Hellblau, then applied RLM 74 Graugrün topside, with a fin and rudder painted in RLM 81 Braunviolett and 82 Dunkelgrün. The RLM 76 Lichtblau bands on the fuselage, wings, and tailplanes were airbrushed freehand. All the exterior colors were mixed from Tamiya acrylics.

After all the painting was done, Alfonso applied a clear gloss coat using Microgloss, then washed all recesses and panel lines with thinned black enamel. A clear flat coat provided the overall final finish.

The Ju 188, with its huge, bulbous greenhouse, makes an oddly attractive model. The banded winter scheme produces added interest, so the overall effort is irresistible.

The cockpit detail is easily seen through the Ju 188's huge greenhouse canopy. Note how the banded camouflage is applied over the canopy framing. Alfonso applied a black wash to all the recessed panel lines.

After painting, the cockpit was transformed. Here, the left cockpit wall has been attached to the tub.

CHAPTER EIGHT

Modeling a late-war Messerschmitt

FINE TUNING REVELL-MONOGRAM'S BF 109G

Messerschmitt Bf 109Gs soldiered on until the end of World War II, sometimes in unusual camouflage schemes like this one.

Few would dispute that Willy Messerschmitt's Bf 109 was synonymous with Germany during World War II. Its development mirrored the Reich's changing fortunes as the war progressed: from record-breaking thoroughbred in the late 1930s to overburdened war horse in 1945. In its later variants it was required to keep up with more advanced Allied designs, and because suitable replacements weren't available in substantial numbers, it was kept in front-line service even as defeat embraced the Third Reich.

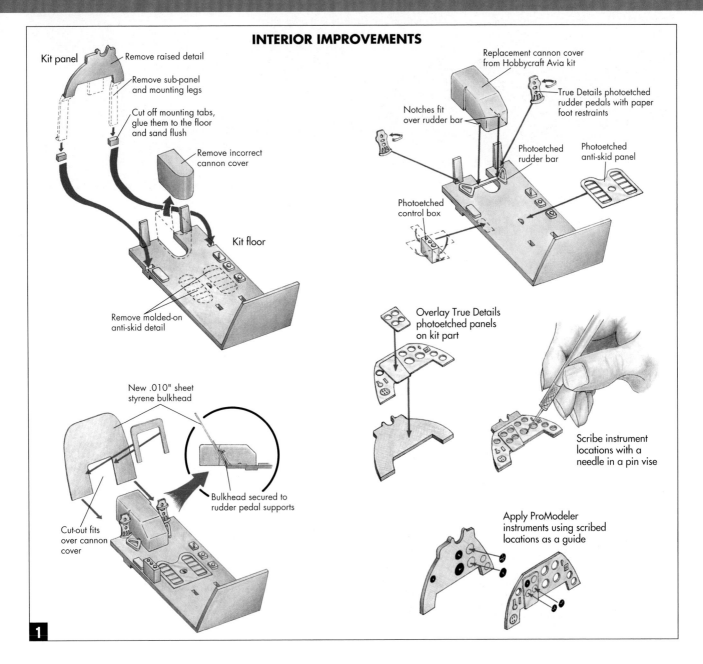

INTERIOR IMPROVEMENTS

Kit panel — Remove raised detail

Remove sub-panel and mounting legs

Cut off mounting tabs, glue them to the floor and sand flush

Remove incorrect cannon cover

Kit floor

Remove molded-on anti-skid detail

New .010" sheet styrene bulkhead

Bulkhead secured to rudder pedal supports

Cut-out fits over cannon cover

Replacement cannon cover from Hobbycraft Avia kit

True Details photoetched rudder pedals with paper foot restraints

Notches fit over rudder bar

Photoetched rudder bar

Photoetched anti-skid panel

Photoetched control box

Overlay True Details photoetched panels on kit part

Scribe instrument locations with a needle in a pin vise

Apply ProModeler instruments using scribed locations as a guide

1

By Jim Green

Most Bf 109 models that I've seen have represented aircraft flown by well known aces (such as Erich Hartmann) or planes from famous fighter units. I decided to build one that would be different—typical of the late-war period, and characterizing the weariness of the Luftwaffe's struggle during the war's last days.

Revell-Monogram's kit was tooled in the late 1970s. Its detail may not rival the best of today's kits, but it's a good late Bf 109G-10. The kit's only shortcomings are a cockpit and land-ing gear that lack detail. But that can be remedied easily with aftermarket items, a few spare parts, and a little creativity.

Cockpit improvements. First, I corrected and detailed the kit's instrument panel and the cockpit floor as outlined in the drawing, **1**. I used True Details' photoetched set No. 48812 along with instrument decals from ProModeler's German fighter instrument sheet. The end result is a vast improvement, **2**. I covered the instrument with drops of white glue, which dries clear and gives the impression of a glass cover.

Photoetched details in place

New bulkhead blanks out forward fuselage

2

The new interior tub looks great when painted.

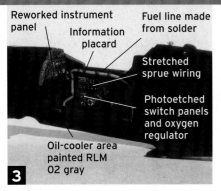

Reworked instrument panel
Information placard
Fuel line made from solder
Stretched sprue wiring
Photoetched switch panels and oxygen regulator
Oil-cooler area painted RLM 02 gray

3 The finished right side of the interior shows the characteristic yellow fuel line.

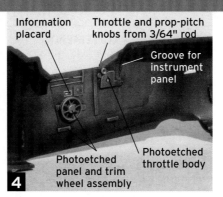

Information placard
Throttle and prop-pitch knobs from 3/64" rod
Groove for instrument panel
Photoetched panel and trim wheel assembly
Photoetched throttle body

4 The left side of the interior shows throttle and controls.

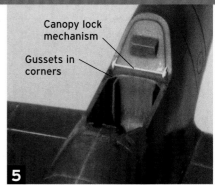

Canopy lock mechanism
Gussets in corners

5 Here the seat has been blended to the deck and the canopy lock mechanism has been added from styrene sheet and wire.

IMPROVING THE REAR DECK

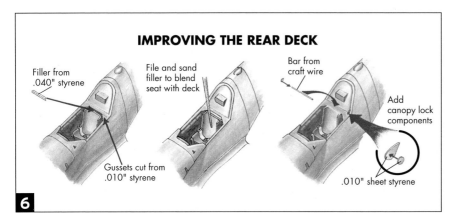

Filler from .040" styrene
File and sand filler to blend seat with deck
Bar from craft wire
Add canopy lock components
Gussets cut from .010" styrene
.010" sheet styrene

6

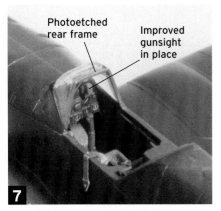

Photoetched rear frame
Improved gunsight in place

7 The kit windscreen received improvements. Note the dangling harness strap.

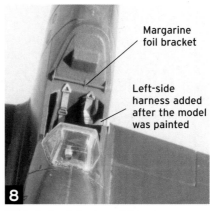

Margarine foil bracket
Left-side harness added after the model was painted

8 The photoetched seat harness was bent to shape.

HEAD ARMOR

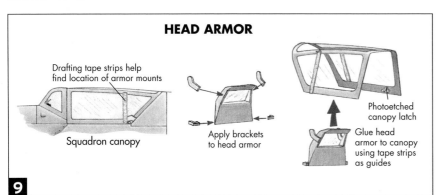

Drafting tape strips help find location of armor mounts
Squadron canopy
Apply brackets to head armor
Photoetched canopy latch
Glue head armor to canopy using tape strips as guides

9

Next, I detailed the cockpit side-walls, 3 and 4. Removing the raised details made way for the new parts. Grooves scored into both fuselage halves accept the rebuilt instrument panel. I have found pilot's accessory catalogs such as Sporty's to be a great source of photos of instruments and placards. I can usually find some that will fit any project.

At this time, I mounted the kit's exhaust stacks and the oil cooler with the photoetched intake screen. I improved the exhaust pipes by making several passes with a knife-edged file to separate the stacks, then drilled them out with a small bit mounted in a pin vise.

Next I applied the photoetched lap belts to the pilot's seat and set that assembly aside for later. The kit's gunsight was replaced with a pair of reflectors made from thin acetate, also set aside for later.

I painted the interior with Testor Model Master enamels. I airbrushed flat black on the floorboard and side walls, then dry-brushed with Euro I dark gray. Individual items were then picked out in appropriate colors: yellow for the fuel line, insignia blue for the oxygen regulator, dry brushed silver for the rudder pedals and bar, and brown for the stick handle and pedal foot restraints. I weathered the finish using brown watercolors and pastels, then picked out worn and scuffed areas with a silver pencil (found in art supply stores). An airbrushed application of Dullcote was the final touch.

Brackets from 1/72 scale German assault gun

10 The finished Galland hood includes the modified head armor.

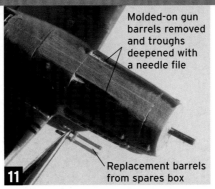

Molded-on gun barrels removed and troughs deepened with a needle file

Replacement barrels from spares box

11 The nose guns were poorly defined in the kit moldings, so improvements helped.

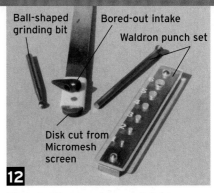

Ball-shaped grinding bit

Bored-out intake

Waldron punch set

Disk cut from Micromesh screen

12 The small supercharger inlet was drilled out and refurbished.

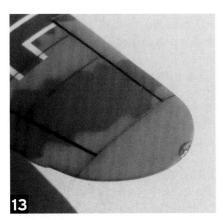

13 New wing-tip navigation lights were made from clear plastic.

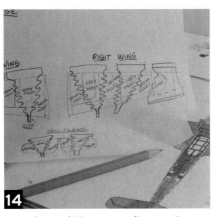

RIGHT WING

14 Drawings of the camouflage scheme were traced onto card stock and used as soft masks.

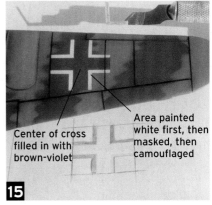

Center of cross filled in with brown-violet

Area painted white first, then masked, then camouflaged

15 On this model, the upper-surface crosses are not decals. Jim painted the white outlines first, then filled in the centers.

Canopy improvements. I had planned from the start to add a Squadron vacuum-formed "Galland hood" canopy to model a late G-10 variant. I also wanted to correct the shape of the cockpit opening.

After assembling the fuselage and mating the wings and tailplane, I filled the gap between the back of the kit's floorboard and the underside of the cockpit decking with a shim of plastic and super glue. I smoothed the joint with a homemade tool of sandpaper strips wrapped around a section of Plastruct I-beam stock, held by angled cross-locking tweezers.

To fashion the proper shape of the cockpit opening, I added .010" sheet triangular gussets to the rear corners and blended them in, **5.** In preparation for painting the back deck, I used an airbrush (with no paint, obviously) to blast sanding dust from the

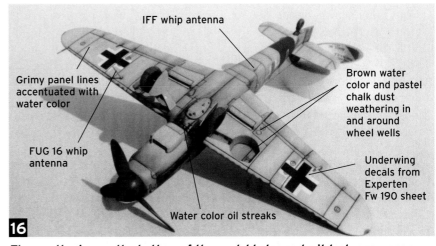

IFF whip antenna

Grimy panel lines accentuated with water color

FUG 16 whip antenna

Brown water color and pastel chalk dust weathering in and around wheel wells

Underwing decals from Experten Fw 190 sheet

Water color oil streaks

16 The weathering on the bottom of the model helps make it look war-weary.

cockpit, then cut drafting tape to size and masked the rear bulkhead below the repaired area. I protected the rest of the cockpit by stuffing in wet tissue and painted the rear deck with flat black, followed with dry-brushed Euro I dark gray.

After unmasking the cockpit, I installed the seat, only to discover the inaccurate step between the top of the seat and the back deck. Since this configuration wouldn't allow the photoetched shoulder harnesses to "hang" properly, I corrected it with a

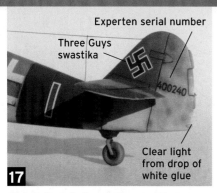

Three Guys swastika
Experten serial number
Clear light from drop of white glue

17

The tail end shows the mottled camouflage of the late-war scheme.

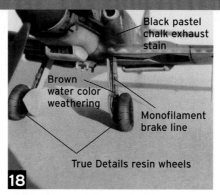

Black pastel chalk exhaust stain
Brown water color weathering
Monofilament brake line
True Details resin wheels

18

Landing gear improvements include new wheels.

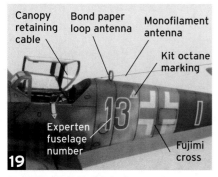

Canopy retaining cable
Bond paper loop antenna
Monofilament antenna
Kit octane marking
Experten fuselage number
Fujimi cross

19

Topside details include radio antennas.

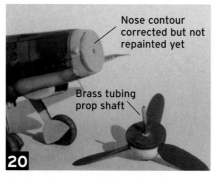

Nose contour corrected but not repainted yet
Brass tubing prop shaft

20

During final assembly, Jim found the nose was malformed.

sheet-styrene shim and filed it smooth. I also added canopy-lock detail from bits of styrene and wire, **6**. The retaining bracket was made from a piece of foil margarine wrapper attached with white glue.

Next, I thinned the inside edge of the kit's windscreen with a knife to accept the photoetched windshield frame, **7**. I wet-sanded and polished the area smooth, cleaned up the residue with a cotton swab and denatured alcohol, then attached the windshield frame with super glue. I mounted the gunsight to the instrument panel, then glued the windscreen to the model. A light sanding blended the rear frame into the windscreen.

After final painting to the cockpit deck, I added the right shoulder harness and pre-bent (but did not install) the left one, **8**. I wanted to drape the left harness over the cockpit sill, so I added it after painting the airframe.

I modified the kit's canopy head armor so it would fit inside Squadron's vacuum-formed canopy,

9. The kit part is designed to fit the thicker injection-molded canopy, so I stole new mounting brackets from a 1/72 scale German assault gun that were wide enough to fit inside the thin vacuum-formed hood, **10**. The armor frame was painted RLM black-gray and attached to the inside of the hood with white glue.

Finished with the cockpit, I masked it and the glass panels of the windscreen and canopy and airbrushed the interior frame color of black-gray.

Exterior enhancements. The kit's gun barrels lacked detail, so I cut them out and deepened the troughs with a needle file, **11**. I found a pair of gun barrels in my spares box and carefully bored out the muzzles with a fine drill bit.

The next item up for the detailer's treatment was the supercharger intake, **12**. After gluing the intake halves together, I filed off the locating tab and bored a hole in the flat side that faces the fuselage. I also bored out the intake with a ball-shaped cut-

ting bit turned between my thumb and forefinger. I used a Waldron punch set to make a screen disc and inserted it into the hole in the flat side. I painted the inside of the intake with RLM 02 gray.

Using a round file, I notched out the wing-tip navigation lights, then cut new ones from the corners of a .040" clear sheet. These were filed and sanded to fit in the notches. I used a fine drill bit to bore a depression in the back side of each lens, and applied a tiny drop of red (left) and green paint to simulate the bulb. I attached the new lenses to the notch with gel-type super glue, then sanded and polished them to clarity, **13**.

Painting. I painted my model as a Reich Defense machine of JG 27 using Testor Model Master enamels. The scheme was RLM 75 gray-violet and RLM 81 brown-violet topsides over RLM 76 light blue. Testors' RLM 81 looked more like Olive Drab, so I used French Chestnut Brown instead.

Before applying the camouflage, though, I painted the wheel wells RLM 02 gray, then painted the nose stripe yellow and the Reich Defense tail band green. Next I painted the area of the upper wing crosses white. Masks cut from signmaker's "Gerber mask" were laid on the white to create the white cross outlines. These stayed on during the application of the camouflage. When all the painting was done the masks were moved to reveal the white-outlined cross.

The first camouflage color to go on was RLM 76 light blue. This served as a primer and made it easier to find surface flaws. The next color was the upper surface RLM 75 gray-violet. The camouflage on the fuselage was not applied to any official pattern and seemed random. I airbrushed RLM 81 brown-violet freehand, extending the dark colors well down the fuselage sides. Each swatch of color ended in a loose, random mottle.

The wing pattern on this machine

was more organized, though, with a soft, wavy sawtooth pattern. I drew scale paper patterns, **14**, cut them out, then traced them onto manila folder card stock. This stiffer material was perfect for making soft masks for the scheme.

The segments of the soft masks were applied to the model with small loops of masking tape to hold them in position and to hold them just off the surface. With the edges of the masks held away from the surface, the airbrush created a definite, yet slightly soft, edge to the pattern, **15**.

I masked around the already-masked white outlines of the upper-surface crosses and filled in with RLM 81.

Decaling and weathering. Color photos of late-war Messerschmitts reveal grime and wear from hard use, inadequate maintenance, and primitive field conditions.

First, I airbrushed Testor Dullcote over the entire model. I enhanced the panel lines with a No. 2 pencil, then dragged a bristle brush over each panel line, smudging the graphite to blend and give a grimy appearance. More Dullcote sealed the graphite to the model. I added another layer of heavy grime to the panel lines using watercolors applied with a fine-point brush. Brown was used in the wheel wells and landing gear; a mixture of brown with a little black for the undersurfaces, **16**; black on the upper surface of the wing and for the panel lines around the engine and in the recesses around the exhaust stacks. The application of black is heaviest at the front of the aircraft.

Once the watercolors were dry, I moistened a cotton swab and wicked away excess watercolor from the panel lines, softening and blending the weathering. Dragging the cotton swab in the direction of the aircraft's slipstream prevents unnatural looking smudges of color. Another application of Dullcote sealed the weathering. Oil streaks behind the oil

Jim's updated Revell-Monogram kit, with its aftermarket parts and extra attention, is a striking representation of one of the Third Reich's final fighters.

cooler were made with undiluted black watercolor and again sealed with Dullcote.

Since decals adhere best to glossy surfaces, I airbrushed Testor Glosscote in the areas that would receive decals. All the decals came from my spares box. The underwing insignia, red fuselage number, and serials came from Experten's Fw 190D sheet; the fuselage crosses with gray centers and the gruppe bar both came from an old Fujimi Bf 109 kit; the Swastikas are from the out-of-print Three Guys Replicas sheet, **17**; the fuel octane symbol is from the Monogram sheet. Once the decals were dry, yet another application of Dullcote restored the flat finish.

Even more weathering was done with dust scraped from artist's pastel chalks. I used brown on the undersides to replicate dried mud stains and dirt. I used black for gunsmoke streaks and exhaust stains. The poor quality fuel used by late-war 109s didn't burn cleanly, so I made the stains really dirty and sooty. Another shot of Dullcote protects the pastel dust.

Itsy bitsies. After unmasking the canopy, I draped the left shoulder harness out of the cockpit. Next I added the underside details; landing gear FUG 16 antenna mast, pitot, aileron mass balances, and the IFF whip antenna. I replaced the kit tires with True Details resin ones and super glued 2.2-lb monofilament brake lines to the struts, **18**. I curled a

bit of fly-tying wire for the end of the FUG 16 antenna and used a nylon paintbrush bristle for the IFF whip.

More 2.2-1b monofilament was used for the radio antenna topside. This was secured into pre-drilled holes with tiny drops of super glue. Waving a heated nail underneath the monofilament made it taut. I added tiny drops of white glue to simulate insulators. The loop antenna on the fuselage spine is a strip of coated bond paper that was curled around a dowel, painted brown-violet, and attached with white glue, **19**.

The canopy was attached with white glue and the joint was over-coated with Dullcote to avoid the glossy glue look. Fly-tying wire was used for the canopy retaining cable.

Just when you think you're finished, something goes wrong. I had left off the propeller, figuring to add it last. Oh no! The spinner backplate didn't match the fuselage; the right "cheek" area of the nose was out-of-round. I ended up having to reshape the nose with emery boards and sandpaper, **20**. I then masked, repainted, and re-weathered the area. The addition of the prop finished the job.

And there you have a Messerschmitt that looks the part of a war-weary Luftwaffe veteran during the Third Reich's final hours.

CHAPTER NINE

Painting a desert-scheme Stuka

A GOOD WAY TO PRODUCE WILD, "FIELD-APPLIED" CAMOUFLAGE

The complicated vein camouflage on this 1/48 scale Hasegawa Ju 87B Stuka is best applied by airbrushing and using masks. Robert Kingsley will show you how.

I've always liked the complicated camouflage schemes used on many Luftwaffe aircraft. As a kid, I tried to duplicate many of these "mottle" and "vein" schemes on my models by using cotton balls and swabs dipped in paint and stippled on the models. In particular, I had a 1/48 scale Ju 87B Stuka that I stippled in a gray and brown desert style based loosely on a black-and-white photo.

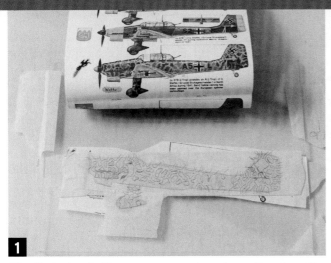

1 The first step in the process was to enlarge the aircraft drawing to the scale of the model. Next, Robert traced the camouflage pattern unto paper, then transferred the marks to masking tape.

2 Since no pattern for the wing was provided in the drawings, Robert adapted the fuselage pattern to maintain the size and style of the masked shaped.

By Robert Kingsley

In retrospect, the model was crude at best, replete with cotton fuzz in the paint, but at the time I thought it looked great. Now, I've recreated my childhood desert-scheme Ju 87B with a new and improved version, this time based on much better information—without the use of cotton!

The camouflage pattern for my Hasegawa Ju 87B was inspired by a color centerspread illustration in Squadron/Signal's *Ju 87 Stuka in Action*. This aircraft is a Ju 87B-2/R-2 Trop (short for "Tropical," or Mediterranean Theater) of 3 Staffel, 1 Gruppe/Stukageschwäder 1, which served in North Africa in 1941.

The aircraft has a complicated vein pattern of RLM 79 sandgelb (sand yellow) sprayed over the standard factory-applied splinter pattern of RLM 71 dunkelgrün (dark green) and RLM 70 schwarzgrün (black green); the undersides are RLM 65 hellblau (light blue).

At first, the addition of sand yellow over the standard dark greens was usually done in the field by ground crews. The idea was to adapt the green European camouflage colors and patterns to a desert environment. Later, Stukas and other aircraft

bound for the Mediterranean campaign had their upper surfaces painted overall yellow at the factory, with green or brown mottles sometimes applied in the field. The Squadron/Signal book illustrates many of these patterns.

I used Floquil for the RLM colors and Testor Model Master for everything else. This aircraft's markings are

reproduced on a Super Scale International decal sheet (No. 48-443).

Hasegawa's Ju 87B-2 kit (No. 09113) served as the basis for my model, though to do it again I would use Hasegawa's "Desert Stuka" kit (No. 09116), since it includes the correct, larger supercharger air intake installed on Trop Stukas. Eduard's Ju 87B detail set (No. 48-129) adds

Masking over decals: risky business

At first, it seems to make sense. Add field-applied camouflage by masking over the original paint and markings, just as was done to the real thing. But model decal markings are fragile, even when overcoated, and they might come off with the mask. Here's why:

Masking materials, even low-tack tape and frisket, can sometimes stick better to a coating than the coating can stick to what is under it. A cross-section of the surface of a finished model is like a layer cake. From the bare plastic upward, there may (or may not) be a layer of primer, a layer of paint, maybe a second or third layer (or color) of paint, a clear gloss overcoat, a decal, maybe another clear gloss overcoat, and a clear flat overcoat.

Masking materials can be aggressive grabbers. If any bond of any layer is weaker than the bond of the tape to the top layer, it can fail and all the layers above it may come off with the tape.

Decal adhesives are potentially the weakest layer of the cake. The tape may stick well to the clear flat overcoat, and the overcoat may stick well to the decal, but if the decal doesn't adhere well to the clear gloss layer beneath, it will peel off, leaving a clean glossy patch exposed.

Test first before trying this on a model, especially if you're using a different brand of paint or decal than you're used to.

- Paul Boyer

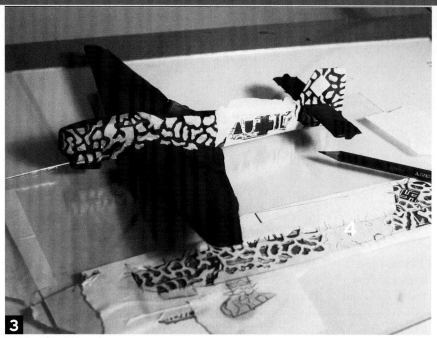

3 Robert applied pieces of the mask individually. He also masked off the position of the markings.

4 With all the masks in place the model is ready to paint. Robert's test strip shows whether the yellow paint would cover the dark camouflage—after several light coats, it did.

tremendous detail to both the exterior and interior.

Paint and paint again. To paint the vein-style camouflage on my Stuka, I first applied the standard splinter scheme, then overlaid the sand yellow veins just the way it was done on the real airplane. Ordinarily, you would want to paint the lighter color first, then add darker colors on top of it. That wouldn't work well here.

Even though the original Stuka may have had its desert camouflage applied with a brush, doing so in this scale would not look good. Airbrushing through a mask is the best way.

From the outset of this project, I was concerned that the lighter yellow wouldn't cover the darker greens well enough, and that the contrast might be too stark. Before I painted my model, I made a test strip using the same paints on a scrap piece of plastic. After painting the splinter scheme on the strip, I varied the desert yellow coverage to evaluate the best effect. Several light coats of the yellow worked best.

Traces. Prior to assembly, trace the outlines of the upper wing and horizontal stabilizer parts onto paper. These will serve as templates for the camouflage masking later.

Build the kit and apply the standard splinter camouflage scheme. Leave off the horizontal stabilizer supports until after painting so you won't accidentally crunch them during the masking (as I did). Spray the light blue underside first and allow it to dry thoroughly, then mask it off and apply the RLM 71 dark green. Hasegawa's kit provides paper templates for the splinter pattern to help make masks from tape or frisket. Mask off the dark green using the templates and apply the RLM 70 black green.

Use an enlarging photocopier to blow up the camouflage drawing (in this case, the Squadron/Signal artwork) to the scale of the model. Make several copies. You'll need them, especially if you're like me and goof up a lot. Also, make a few copies (at 100 percent) of the decal sheets too; you'll need to cut masks to cover the areas that will receive decals, too.

Trace the pattern style from the drawing onto masking material. The best way is to trace directly onto frisket film. This translucent, paper-backed self-adhesive film comes in sheets or rolls and is available in art-supply stores. Badger Air-Brush Co. also markets sheets in hobby shops.

Since I didn't have frisket, I did it the hard way—tracing the pattern onto wide swaths of masking tape applied to a sheet of glass, **1.** To see the pattern, I placed the enlarged

SOURCES
Photoetched details Eduard, Obrnice 170, 43521 Obrnice, Czech Republic, www.eduard.cz
Decals Superscale International, 2360 Apache Drive, Bishop, CA 93514, www.superscale.com

REFERENCES
Ju 87 Stuka in Action Brian Filley, Squadron/Signal Publications, Carrollton, Texas
Junkers Ju 87 Ulrich Elfrath, Schiffer Military History, Atglen, Pennsylvania
Warplanes of the Luftwaffe edited by David Donald, Aerospace Publishing Ltd., London, England
Stuka: Dive Bombers - Pursuit Bombers - Combat Pilots Gerhard Aders and Werner Held, Schiffer Publishing, Ltd. Atglen, Pennsylvania

Here's a close look at the finished veined camouflage. Note the standard camouflage "beneath" the veins, and how the veins work around the German cross and codes. The canopy frames did not receive the sand-yellow veins, but most of the stencils were overpainted.

drawing underneath the glass and on top of an artist's light table.

Since the pattern in the drawing showed only the left side of the airplane, I created the right side by flopping the drawing over and tracing it again onto the mask. What about the topside? Who knows! I used the fuselage pattern as a guide to the size and shape of the pattern elements and cut masks for the wing and stabilizers, **2**. The wheel spats were handled in the same fashion.

Unlike the fuselage sides, don't simply flop the pattern from one wing to the other. Since you'll be able to see both wings at once, the mirror image would be too obvious.

Over, under, around, and through. The tricky part on this aircraft is that the vein pattern didn't extend under any of the larger markings, because they were applied earlier on top of the factory paint. Most likely, smaller markings and stencils were overpainted.

According to the Squadron/Signal drawing, the two octane-specification triangles on the left side and the "diving crow" emblems on both sides of the nose were either avoided or reapplied. These features may not be relevant to all Stukas, so check your references for the aircraft you plan to build.

When it came to painting around the markings, I couldn't replicate the original process. The original markings were either masked over or carefully avoided by the field painter. If I had applied the decals over the splinter scheme, I would have risked damaging them with the mask. I established the positions of the crosses, swastikas, and codes by making a photocopy of the decal sheet and tracing their shapes onto masking tape.

Applying the masks. With all the patterns drawn on the frisket or masking tape, use a sharp blade to cut out each piece of the mask. Though tedious, the results will make it all worthwhile. When you have all the pieces cut, transfer them to the model one at a time, **3**.

Lift each piece by picking up a corner with a sharp blade, then burnish the mask on the model. Remember you are masking the areas that will not get the sand yellow veining—you are applying masks for all the irregular blobs in between the veins.

You may have to make new pieces of mask to go over the top of the fuselage, so cut these freehand from masking material. Don't worry about accuracy; remember, the pattern was random. Just make sure you have no overly large green areas or overly large yellow veins.

Coverage. Before you apply the vein camouflage, make sure all the masks are sticking and burnish them if needed, **4**. Spray on the yellow in light, even coats, letting each set up before applying the next. This will prevent flooding, which can creep under the masks and create thick edges around the pattern.

Removing the masks. To avoid scratching the paint, carefully pick up one edge of each masked blob with a dull hobby knife. Lift up just enough to grab each blob with tweezers. To reduce the risk of lifting the paint, pull the tape backward at an angle as close to 180 degrees as possible.

Once all the masks are removed, check the paint job for missed spots or creeping paint and retouch as necessary. When everything is dry, you can gloss, decal, and overcoat with clear flat.

This painting method is time-consuming, but it gives crisp, clean lines, deep color, and an accurate look you can be proud of—without cotton-ball fuzz.

CHAPTER TEN

Detailing Hasegawa's Me 163B

BRING OUT THE BEAUTY OF THIS 1/32 SCALE KOMET

The rocket-powered Komet packed a punch, and William Steidl's model is packed with detail, most of it scratchbuilt.

The Messerschmitt 163B Komet made its debut in 1941 as the world's first (and only) rocket-powered fighter. Though hard to handle and often dangerous to its pilots, it remains one of the most intriguing aircraft ever conceived—and a popular model subject. I build in 1/32 scale, and saw an opportunity to improve the Hasegawa kit by adding plenty of realistic detail—most of it scratchbuilt.

By William A Steidl
Photos by the author

As it is with most 1/32 scale projects, selecting the particular markings for my Komet was a challenge. Eventually, my resources on the Me 163B led me to build W.Nr191659—it required the least amount of alterations, had the nicest color scheme, and Super Scale International offered decals (at the time, anyway).

To keep the project organized and give myself some sense of accomplishment, I divided the model into subassemblies: the cockpit, the landing gear, the engine, and the fuselage.

Constructing the cockpit. First, I collected all of the kit's cockpit parts and dry-fitted them. This gave me ideas about the relative space between items and where there would be room for additional detail. Then I pulled out my reference material and decided which parts were going to stay and which parts weren't.

I removed the cockpit tub's raised detail, which was mostly the strapping for the T-Stoff fuel tanks (located on either side of the tub) and the radio panel. I then added my own scratchbuilt strapping, **1**, and radio panel, **2**. The armor plate from the kit was just fine, plus it ensured a good fit within the fuselage. From there I moved on to the oxygen regulator, which I also decided to rebuild, **3**.

The trim control box and hand wheel were rebuilt using styrene, a plastic washer, and stretched sprue, **4**. I modified the kit's control stick by running wire along the length of the shaft (secured with lead foil), using foil to make a machine-gun trigger at the top of the handle.

The Komet's gun sight is conspicuous, so I wanted mine to look its best. I started out with 1/32" sheet styrene and cut my two basic blocks using the kit part as reference for dimensions. I then drilled a 1/16" hole, painted the edges silver, filled it with epoxy, and then topped it off with a Waldron instrument bezel. The second block was then attached to the

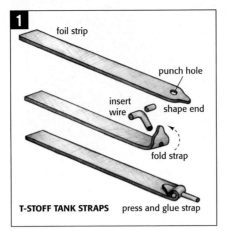

T-STOFF TANK STRAPS

William made strapping for the T-Stoff tanks from lead foil strips and 24-gauge wire. After the straps were in place and the cockpit was painted, he removed paint from the straps with dirty black thinner.

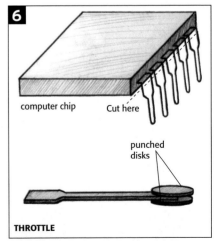

OXYGEN REGULATOR

William built the replacement oxygen regulator from styrene and wrapped wire, securing the ends of the wire with a thin strip of foil and making a connection-like assembly.

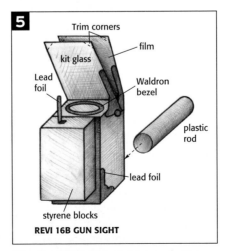

REVI 16B GUN SIGHT

The Revi 16B gun sight was built using sheet styrene for the basic block, drilling out the lens hole, filling it with epoxy, and adding a bezel.

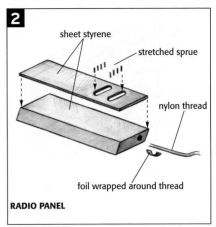

RADIO PANEL

The replacement radio panel was topped with a 1/64" sheet containing cutouts for switches, made by punching out 1/32" diameter holes at either end of the slot and cutting out the pieces between the holes.

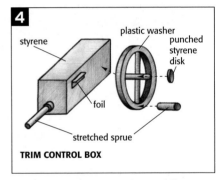

TRIM CONTROL BOX

For this trim control box, William used materials that gave him the look he wanted. Lead foil, still found on some wine bottles, proved to be a handy material for this project.

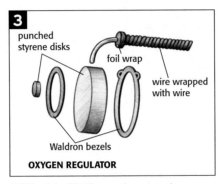

THROTTLE

Throttles are easy to make—just attach two 1/32" diameter disks of .015" styrene sheet to either side of a computer chip "leg."

7

William filled every available space in the cockpit with carefully planned details. Skillful dry-brushing makes the details stand out realistically.

8

The kit includes only a basic wheel dolly. Since you can't just pull one of these out of your spares box, careful research is essential to getting it right.

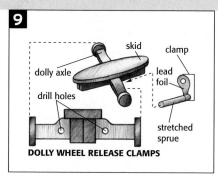

9

skid
clamp
dolly axle
lead foil
drill holes
stretched sprue

DOLLY WHEEL RELEASE CLAMPS

The dolly clamps were made by folding a rectangle of lead foil in half, cutting out a teardrop shape, then inserting a ⅟₁₆"-diameter rod through the unfolded shape.

10

In the kit part, the tail wheel and the fork were molded as one. William's replacement makes a dramatic difference.

REFERENCES
The Official Monogram Painting Guide To German Aircraft 1935-1945 Kenneth A. Merrick, Monogram Aviation Publications, Boylston, Massachusetts, 1980
German Aircraft Interiors 1935-1945 Vol. 1 Kenneth A. Merrick, Monogram Aviation Publications, Sturbridge, Massachusetts, 1996
Aero Detail 10: Messerschmitt Me 163 and Heinkel He 162 Nohara and Shiwaku, Dai-Nippon Kaiga Publishing, Japan, 1994
Messerschmitt Me 163 "Komet" Vol. 2 M. Emmerling and J. Dressel, Schiffer Publishing, West Chester, Pennsylvania, 1992
Cockpit Donald Nijboer, Howell Press, Charlottesville, VA, 1998

SOURCES
Photoetched detail parts, punch set Waldron Model Products, P.O. Box 431, Merlin, OR 97532, 503-474-1159
Decals Super Scale International, 2360 Apache Drive, Bishop, CA 93514, www.superscale.com

first, keeping the left sides flush. The kit glass was used for the reflector plate and some old film for the tinted glass plate. I finished the gun sight by cutting and attaching lead foil as a frame for the glass, **5**.

I used the kit's main instrument panel as a guide for constructing a new and improved panel out of styrene. First, I marked where the gauges would go, punched the holes, and painted the panel. After it dried, I punched and placed the appropriate Waldron dial face in each of the holes, and then glued from the back—a very clean method.

I finished the panel by gluing Waldron instrument bezels around each of the dial faces, and then dry-brushed them. I used stretched sprue for switches and black wire for knobs. I like to pre-drill all of my switch locations (I prefer a No. 80 thumb drill), insert the sprue, and then glue from behind. Old com-

puter chips can be recycled into great throttle levers—just snip a "leg" off the chip and attach ⅟₃₂"-diameter punched disks (from .015" sheet styrene) to either side, **6**.

To improve the cockpit seat I rounded off its corners, added seat belts and buckles from Waldron, and formed a seat cushion from clay, **7**. I finished off the cockpit by adding some ribbing to the sides of the fuselage using lead foil, some fuel lines using lead wire, and two more levers for the canopy release and tow cable release.

Here's a little trick: Glue the cockpit tub to one side of the fuselage and the instrument panel to the other side. They won't interfere with one another when they are glued, and it's much easier to glue the instrument panel to the fuselage.

The canopy was lined with lead foil on both sides, and an air intake hole was added to the front. Not all of the

Me 163s have this air intake at the front of the canopy, so you'll need to check references for the particular plane you're building.

Landing gear. The landing gear was modified by adding a dolly release mechanism and a reinforced skid plate, **8**. The kit has no detail on how the wheel dolly gets attached to the skid in real life—the dolly is missing two clamps from its detail and the skid lacks a release mechanism. The clamps attach to protruding rods on either side of the skid. The idea was for the rods to retract after takeoff, releasing the dolly. The clamps made from stretched sprue and lead foil, **9**, were attached to the dolly axle by drilling out holes on either side.

Since the kit's tail wheel was molded into the fork, I completely rebuilt the whole assembly, **10**. I modeled it first in thick paper following my references as a guide, then

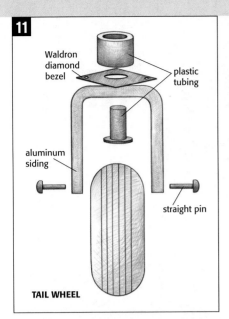

Waldron
diamond
bezel

plastic
tubing

aluminum
siding

straight pin

TAIL WHEEL

After a fork made of plastic sheet proved too weak to support the weight of the plane, William rebuilt the tail-wheel fork from leftover parts of aluminum siding trim.

transferred the template over to aluminum and drilled out all of the holes. Next, I bent the aluminum into its proper shape. It was strong enough, but didn't take well to gluing, so I drilled a hole through the center of the fork and ran a capped plastic rod from the bottom, through the hole and into a plastic tube above, **11**. The arm connecting the tail wheel to the plane was cut from plastic stock using the kit-supplied part as a guide for thickness.

Engine. The engine was built from the kit parts, but then I went on a wiring frenzy and added all the engine lines I could, **12**. The sad part is that no one will ever see all the work done to the engine because I elected to glue the front and rear sections of the fuselage together!

Finishing the fuselage. I sanded off all the raised detail on the fuselage and the wings, and re-scribed the entire plane. This took a while and I highly suggest to anyone who is thinking about doing such a job to perform this task while the wings and elevators are not yet joined. It just makes the job so much easier because everything can be just laid down flat and scribed. I created a set of tem-

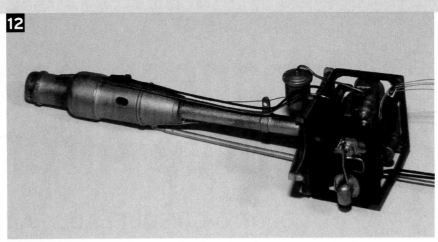

The engine was finished according to references, including all the wiring. You can't see it on the finished model, but it's in there.

plates for scribing the irregularly shaped hatches.

Using Testor Model Master enamel paints, I custom blended each of the colors, matching the paint chips supplied in Merrick & Hitchcock's book (see references). The Luftwaffe's camouflage scheme called for a splinter pattern of RLM 81/82 (brown-violet/dark green) on all upper surfaces, and RLM 76 (light blue) for the tail and under surfaces. I switched from a single-action to a dual action airbrush to apply a mottling pattern of RLM 81/82 to the tail. I stenciled and sprayed all the markings except for the two "15"s, which were decals. The

production numbers and fuel type letters were dry transfers.

An ordinary lead pencil was used to darken the panel lines; following up with pastels provided the shading. The entire model then got a coat of Testor Model Master clear flat, which provided the proper sheen.

I had a lot of fun building this kit, but it wouldn't have been possible without a little help from my friends. Harry Short supplied me with a wealth of reference material, and Fred Moglia of F&M Hobbies went out of his way to get me all of the materials I requested—I thank them both.

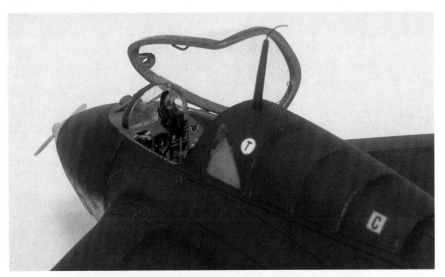

The Komet, equipped with a mismatch of slow guns and a rocket-powered engine, was a technological dead end but an impressive sight over German skies.

CHAPTER ELEVEN

Japanese Army Air Force Aircraft

COLOR & CAMOUFLAGE PAINT GUIDE

A Ki-45 Nick of the 4th Sentai, 2nd Chutai sports a late-war veined scheme, which is actually evenly spaced live green patches sprayed over light gray-green. 1/72 scale models by Harvey Low, photos by Richard Briggs.

During World War II, the Imperial Army Air Force of Japan displayed some of the most vivid markings of the war. Its brilliant Hinomaru (rising-sun insignia), bright identification strips, home defense bands, and Sentai (group) heraldry served as recognition aids and reinforced each unit's bushido, or traditional military honor.

A Ki-2 1-11 Sally shows typical markings of late 1943: yellow wing ID strips, red-brown spinners, and propeller blades with yellow warning bands. Note the red propeller warning strip on the nose.

Another Nick in typical home-defense colors. Although the upper surface appears dark green, it is densely sprayed green over light gray-green. The spinners are red coinciding with the 2nd Chutai.

By Harvey Low

While Japanese Army Air Force (JAAF) color schemes were meant to conceal, their unique combinations of garish markings and functional camouflage resulted in intriguing paint schemes. As with any standard, however, there were exceptions to the rule.

Color chronology. Before the Sino-Japanese Conflict in 1937, biplanes and early monoplanes of the JAAF were painted overall light gray (sometimes called pale gray). As the war with China escalated, an overall light gray-green emerged that eventually became standard factory finish for combat aircraft. However, the need for more effective camouflage became increasingly obvious. Many bombers operating over China and Manchuria had their topsides camouflaged with segmented browns and greens. Light gray or light gray-green remained prevalent on fighter and reconnaissance types.

This segmented camouflage color scheme continued into the early years of WWII—especially on fighters—but light gray-green remained standard factory finish until about 1942. By then, many aircraft were emerging in natural metal, or with a topside camouflage of dark or olive green, to help conceal planes as combat moved over the jungles of the Pacific.

Primary trainers throughout the war were painted orange-red, while advanced trainers (aircraft operating in the dual role of trainer and interceptor) remained light gray, light gray-green, or natural metal. After 1943, trainers often wore mottled finishes of dark or olive green over natural metal, or applied over orange-red.

During the war, segmented camouflage patterns and overall light gray/gray-green colors gradually were superseded by mottled schemes of greens or browns painted randomly over the original base color.

As the JAAF moved to the defense of the home islands in late 1944, single-color upper-surface finishes of darker greens, grays, and khaki browns emerged, along with examples painted in overall dark green or reddish-brown. Ironically, these low-vis schemes often were adorned with brightly colored flashes, stripes, and white defense bands characterizing kamikazes or interceptors. Let's look at each camouflage scheme in detail.

Single overall color scheme. There were four basic single-color paint schemes:

1. Aircraft serving in China, Manchuria, and throughout the early years of WWII wore overall light (pale) gray or the more common light gray-green. Examples include Ki-10 Perry, Ki-27 Nate, Ki-30 Ann, Ki-48 Lily, and Ki-51 Sonia

2. Trainers operated in overall orange-red with black cowlings. Typical examples are the Ki-9 Spruce and Ki-55 Ida.

3. By 1944, low-visibility black-green or red-brown was sometimes used on Kamikaze, interceptor, and high-altitude reconnaissance types such as Ki-45 Nick and Ki-46 Dinah.

4. While not a camouflage color, white was hastily applied to some aircraft in 1945 to comply with Allied surrender terms; green crosses were applied over or near the existing Hinomaru. The white was prone to weathering, resulting in various off-white shades.

I have not found conclusive evidence to confirm overall black thought to be used on some Ki-44 Tojos of the 87th Sentai, and Ki-84 Franks of the 57th Special Attack Unit. It is more likely that these aircraft were painted black-green.

Segmented scheme. Common between 1938 and 1942, the China scheme (or cloud scheme) consisted of two, three, or four colors sprayed randomly to upper surfaces and fixed-landing-gear spats of light gray or light gray-green aircraft. Sometimes, areas of the base color were not overpainted and were integrated into the camouflage. Colors included dark and medium browns, and dark and olive greens.

Occasionally, the colors were separated by thin blue lines to simulate

REFERENCES
Camouflage & Markings of Imperial Japanese Army Fighters (No. 329), Model Art Co. Ltd., Japan, 1989
Eagles of the Rising Sun Dr. Keishiro Nagao, AeroMaster Decals, Miami, Florida, 1995
Famous Airplanes of the World (various issues) Bunrin-Do, Japan
Japanese Army Air Force Camouflage and Markings–World War II Donald W. Thorpe, Aero Publishers Inc., Fallbrook, California, 1968
Japanese Army Aircraft Colours & Markings in the Pacific War–and Before Ian K. Baker, Camberwell, Victoria, Australia, 1992
Koku-Fan Special–The Japanese Army Wings of the Second World War Burin-Do, Japan, date unknown
Koku-Fan Special–Imperial Japanese Army Aircraft 93-4, No. 69, Burin-Do, Japan, 1993
Koku-Fan Special–Japanese Military Aircraft Illustrated (Volumes 1, 2, and 3) Burin-Do, Japan, 1983

This Ki-49 Helen features fine squiggles sprayed over pale blue-gray. Note the camouflage overspray on the edges of all the Hinomaru (rising sun insignia).

rivers in the terrain these aircraft flew over. Examples of the segmented scheme are found often on Ki-21 Sally and Ki-15 Babs. Later in the war, two-color schemes (greens and browns) were more prevalent, as found on Ki-43 Oscar, Ki-48 Lily, and Ki-49 Helen.

Mottled scheme. Most common in 1943 and 1944 throughout every region of operation, this scheme featured random blotches, stripes, and squiggles sprayed or hand-brushed over the base color on the aircraft's upper surfaces.

The camouflage was applied everywhere except on the Hinomaru, no-skid walkways, wing ID strips, and antiglare panels—canopy frames were sometimes excluded, too. Variation was enormous, with some sprayed examples showing extreme artistic finesse, while others were crude field applications.

The colors were dark or olive greens, with medium and earth browns found in the China-Burma theater. Special patterns worthy of note were the veined Ki-45 Nicks of the 4th Sentai, zebra-striped Ki-49 Helens of the 61st Sentai, Italian-style netting applied to some Ki-34 Thoras and Ki-109s, and the many snake-weave-patterned Ki-21 Sallys operating over the jungles of the Pacific. All types from fighters to transports could be seen wearing mottled schemes. Unit and identification markings (except for small stencils) usually were reapplied once the camouflage was finished.

Single upper-surface color scheme. This scheme consisted of single color sprayed onto all upper surfaces. It often wrapped around the leading edges of the wings and tail planes. The division between upper- and lower-surface colors was fairly low and hard-edged. Although the demarcation was relatively smooth and straight, some exceptions were wavy, as seen on a few Ki-102 Randys.

This scheme was found as early as 1942 on Ki-43-Is, finished in dark or olive green upper surfaces. In 1944 and 1945, more functional low-visibility colors were used: black-green, deep olive green, olive brown-green, khaki-drab brown, and red-brown. A few types could even be seen wearing a dark violet-gray (no FS equivalent; also reported as "brown-gray," it could have been weathered khaki- drab brown).

Some wore dark or medium gray (Mitsubishi used a variety of grays on its Ki-67 Peggys), or even medium blue (on Ki-43 Oscars of the 20th Sentai and Ki-51 Sonias of 49th Independent Flying Company). Underside colors remained light gray, light gray-green, natural metal, or in some cases pale blue-gray.

For many manufacturers, this scheme became standard delivery finish during those desperate years. Nakajima, for example, began painting its Oscars and Franks in khaki-drab brown in late '44. In the latter half of the war, some trainers also could be seen with a hastily applied upper-surface coat of olive green over the original orange-red color.

Natural metal. Unpainted skins were common between 1941 and '43. Nakajima delivered its first Ki-43, Ki-44, Ki 49, and Ki-84 aircraft in natural metal, while Kawasaki followed with its Ki-61 Tony. Only the Hinomaru, black antiglare panel(s), no-skid walkways, and (in 1943) the wing ID strips were painted before shipment.

Fabric-covered control surfaces were painted in aluminum dope, or more commonly light gray-green. Once delivered, mottled camouflage schemes often were applied over the natural metal. By 1944, single-color upper-surface camouflage increasingly began to be applied at the factory, leaving the undersides in original bare metal—virtually all Ki-100s were delivered in this manner. However, some aircraft were never delivered in natural metal—notably the Ki-21 Sally and Ki-54 Hickory.

Other color details. The Hino-

COLOR	Nearest FS 595b*	Aero-Master enamel	Gunze Sangyo acrylic	Humbrol enamels	Polly Scale Acrylic	Tamiya acrylic	Testor Model Master enamel
UPPER-SURFACE CAMOUFLAGE							
Dark green	34092		H302	149	505246		1764
Olive green	34098	9093		86	505272		1714
Dark brown	30045	9103	H84	98	505300	XF-10	2096
Medium brown	30117	9096	H37	186	505366	XF-64	1701
Earth brown	30215	9034	H66	62	505320	XF-52	
Medium blue	35183	9004		25	505216	XF-8	2032
Orange-red	32473		H14	82	505356		
LATE YEARS (1944, 1945)							
Black green	34052	9023	H65	75	505314	XF-61	
Deep Olive green	34095	9042	H340	105	505354	XF-13	2114
Olive Brown-green	34088	9092	H78	155	505360	XF-58	1711
Khaki-Drab brown	30118		H72	142	505252		1702
Red-brown (1)	30109		H47	180	505276	XF-9	2007
Dark gray	36076	9022	H301	79	505382	XF-24	1788
Medium gray	36270	9053	H306	126	505384	XF-19	1725
UNDERSIDE/OVERALL CAMOUFLAGE							
Light "pale" gray	36622	9056	H311	28	505394	XF-14	1733
Light gray-green	34424	9095	H62				2115
Pale blue-gray	35526	9101	H67		505248		
OTHER MARKINGS							
Yellow ID strips	32544		H24			XF-6	
Yellow propeller tips	33538	9097	H329	154	505282		1708 or 2118

*First number in the FS595b indicates reflectance (1=gloss, 2=semigloss, 3=flat)
(1) Also used on propellers, spinners, antennas, and as a primer.

maru is a topic of much confusion in terms of its size, placement, color, and the use of white outlining. The size and placement of the Hinomaru varied depending on the aircraft. The insignia were consistently found in all six positions (both sides of the wing, and fuselage) before 1937 and after 1941. Between 1937 and early 1942, the fuselage Hinomaru were absent on virtually all JAAF aircraft.

In terms of its color, there is speculation that there was only one shade (close to FS 31105 or FS 31136). This weathered to a lighter matte shade, which explains why the underside Hinomaru sometimes remained more intense. The Hinomaru also appeared darker when applied over or near dark camouflage colors.

The use of white outlining adds yet another level of complexity. The wing Hinomaru generally remained unoutlined when applied with early segmented finishes. By mid-1943 however, a 75mm white surround began to appear around the fuselage Hinomaru.

Outlined fuselage Hinomaru coincided with the standardization of yellow wing ID strips, but application varied depending on the camouflage scheme, manufacturer, and aircraft type. For example, aircraft in natural metal, light gray/gray-green, or orange-red finishes were less likely to have outlined Hinomaru. Most Ki-27 Nates and Ki-67 Peggys were delivered without outlines. The use of outlined Hinomaru on the wing undersides was rare.

Toward the end of the war, painting out the white outline with dark green or black was not common in the JAAF as compared to their naval counterparts.

Wing identification strips. By mid-1942, Ki-27 Nates of the home-based 244th and 246th Sentais wore brightly colored strips painted on the leading inboard edges of the wings to help in identification by friendly forces. This color could have been red. Some foreign aircraft shipped to Japan for evaluation such

A Ki-44 Tojo of the Akeno Flight School in 1944. Aircraft serving the dual role of defense and training often wore mottled camouflage over natural metal.

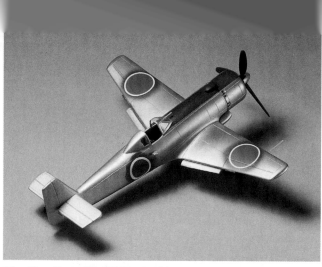

The Kamikaze Ki-115 Tsurugi in overall natural metal (the rear sections were made of wood and painted aluminum color). The dark green surrounds of the Hinomaru were factory applied to expedite the field application of green to the rest of the aircraft

as the Bf 109E also wore red identification strips.

By mid-1943, both the Imperial Army and Navy applied a standard yellow for the wing ID strips. Virtually all aircraft received these markings, with some ID strips painted over portions of the gear doors (as on Ki-43, Ki-61, and Ki-100). The colors ranged from pale yellow to yellow-ochre. Manufacturers' shades varied slightly: Kawasaki's was a rich yellow, while Nakajima had deep orange-yellow. The length of the strip varied depending upon the aircraft.

Home-defense bands. Employed on the home front as early as 1942, broad white bands surrounding the Hinomaru were wrapped around each wing and fuselage. These helped identify the aircraft as friendlies. The width of the bands depended on the aircraft, and photos show they were some times crudely applied. The 47th Sentai and a few flight schools used yellow bands, but this practice was not widespread.

Home-defense bands were not applied on new aircraft toward the end of the war. Some aircraft even had their bands oversprayed with mottled camouflage in the final days of the conflict.

Black cowls and antiglare panels. Black was applied to cowls as early as

the mid-1930s. Its use during the China Incident and WWII, however, was not as common as in the Navy. Its only widespread use was on training aircraft (Ki-9 Spruce, Ki-17 Cedar, and Ki-55 Ida), and some reconnaissance types (Ki-15 Babs and Ki-76 Stella).

Black antiglare panels were applied at the factory. Some sources speculate that Nakajima's black had a blue tinge. In any case, the original paint quickly discolored with heat and weathering to gray-black.

Antiglare panels were applied forward of the canopy along the nose decking, and usually on the inside of the nacelles of multiengine aircraft. Some aircraft (notably Ki-27 Nate, Ki-43-III Oscar, Ki-45 Nick, and Ki-48 Lily) had no antiglare panels.

The use of antiglare panels declined after 1943, when single-color, upper-surface or overall camouflage schemes became more prevalent.

Propellers. Until 1942, front faces of propeller blades usually were polished metal with a 50mm-wide red warning band positioned 50mm from the tip. The rear faces usually were matte black with no markings.

Around 1942, red-brown came into widespread use as the overall color for propellers. Warning bands were yellow instead of red, sometimes on the rear faces as well. Shortly

thereafter, some props had the entire tips painted yellow on both side of the blade. After 1943, some Nakajima aircraft (such as the Ki-43-III Oscar and Ki-84 Frank) had deep-green propellers (close to FS 34128) with yellow tips.

Spinners were painted to three standards: a match of the exterior color of the aircraft; overall red-brown; or the entire spinner or portions of it in Chutai (company) colors—white = 1st company, red = 2nd company, yellow = 3rd company, green = 4th company, blue = headquarters.

Using the color table. The table cross-references the colors described in this article to popular hobby paints. Not every color used by the JAAF is listed, only the most widely cited. Since no official Japanese paint regulations survived the war, positive identification of colors is impossible. Use this cross-reference as a guide, not as a bible. Refer to the references for more detailed analysis of color variations.

Where applicable, I used U.S. Federal Standard 595b color numbers, but don't interpret these as exact matches. The lack of standards and the variations in manufacturing and weathering make determining Japanese colors an inexact science.

Aircraft of the Rising Sun

AN ALL-1/72 SCALE COLLECTION OF JAPANESE WARPLANES

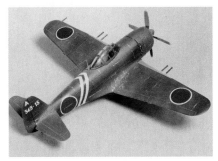

The Shidenkai (George) was an unpleasant surprise to American pilots when first encountered in 1944. This Hasegawa model represents an aircraft of the 343rd Kokutai in 1945.

This Hasegawa model of the A6M5 Zero-sen Model 52 is in the markings of the 201st Kokutai's Shikishima Kamikaze unit, Philippines, 1944. The control surfaces and flaps were cut out and repositioned, and the model was weathered extensively with pastel chalks. Photos by Richard Briggs.

The Nakajima Ki-27 Nate was the Japanese Army's first low-wing monoplane fighter. The model was built from the old Mania kit and is one of Harvey's "quick builds"—it took him only three days from start to completion!

Toronto, Ontario's, **Harvey Low** works in 1/72 scale in part because of manageable model size, acceptable detail, and the challenge of building small models. But mostly he prefers it because of the wide variety of subjects available.

Harvey's P1Y1 Frances, a late-war medium bomber, built from the old Revell kit. It represents an aircraft of the 761st Kokutai naval air corps.

Harvey, a policy and research analyst for the city of Toronto, started modeling in 1974. He recalls his first plastic model, "A 1/48 scale Spitfire with about 10 parts!" A Matchbox Zero with multicolored plastic introduced him to 1/72 scale, and now he seldom builds models in any other scale.

About one of every three models Harvey builds is a conversion or a superdetailed job. The others are straight from the box, allowing him to concentrate on interesting and complicated paint jobs. Harvey prefers airbrushing acrylics thinned with three parts isopropyl alcohol to one part paint. By spraying between 10 and 15 psi, he can airbrush ultra-fine lines. Most of the weathering he does is with artist's pastel chalks.

This Ki-43-II Oscar is decorated for the Royal Thai Air Force, 1944. The camouflage scheme consists of finely sprayed stripes of olive green and earth brown, leaving slivers of the undersurface natural metal showing through. The Hasegawa kit was rescribed, with a new vacuum-formed canopy added. The Thai markings were taken from the 1960s Revell Oscar kit.

CHAPTER THIRTEEN

Modeling the first Ace Sabre

CONVERTING FUJIMI'S F-86F TO AN F-86A

Despite having no individual aircraft markings save the serial number, Capt. James Jabara's ace F-86A is still a striking fighter jet.

Just mention the Korean War to an aircraft enthusiast and visions come to mind of F-86 Sabres tangling with those dreaded MiG-15s. Certainly, the F-86 Sabre has been well represented in the modeling community, but almost every kit available is of the late F-86F with its improved wing and tail surfaces. In 1/72 scale, only the old toy-like Matchbox kit represents the early F-86A.

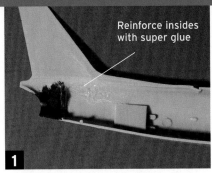

1 Paul used gap-filling super glue to reinforce the inside of the rear fuselage in case the grinding bit in the motor tool should break through the plastic.

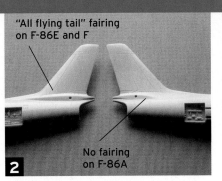

2 The all-flying tail fairing is a noticeable feature of late Sabres. The unmodified Fujimi F-86F fuselage is on the left, while Paul's modified F-86A fuselage is on the right.

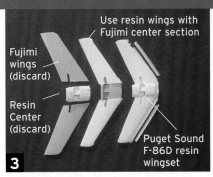

3 Paul used an out-of-production resin slatted wing for this conversion. The center group is the new modified wing.

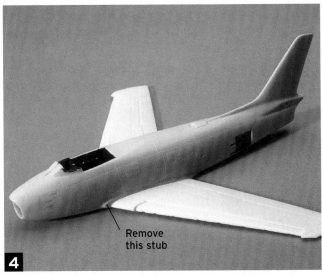

4 The new wing is attached to the fuselage. Note the small leading-edge stub that must be removed.

REFERENCES
F-86 Sabre in Action Larry Davis, Squadron/Signal Publications, Carrollton, Texas, 1992
The North American Sabre Ray Wagner, MacDonald Aircraft Monographs, Doubleday, Garden City, New York, 1963
Warbird History, F-86 Sabre, History of the Sabre and FJ Fury Robert F. Dorr, Motorbooks, Osceola, Wisconsin, 1993
Warbird Tech, North American F-86 SabreJet Day Fighters Kris Hughes and Walter Dranem, Specialty Press, North Branch, Minnesota, 1996
Walkaround F-86 Sabre Larry Davis, Squadron/Signal Publications, Carrollton, Texas, 2000

SOURCES
After my project was finished, the following resin conversion sets for 1/48 and 1/72 scale sabres were announced by **Cutting Edge Models,** Meteor Productions, P.O. Box 3956, Merrifield, VA 22116, 703-971-0500 www.meteorprod.com
F-86A set, CEC48196 and CEC72014
F-86E (early) set (V windscreen and new wing leading edge with separate dropped slats), CEC48197 and CEC72015
F-86E (late) set (new wing leading edge with separate dropped slats), CEC48198 and CEC72016

By Paul Boyer
Photos by Jim Forbes

So, how do you build an accurate early Sabre? The 1/72 scale Fujimi kit I built started life as an F-86F-30 with the "6-3" wing. Here's a list of the changes I had to make:
•Reshape the rear fuselage to eliminate the tailplane actuator fairings
•Backdate the wing to the early narrow chord style with authentic leading-edge slats
•Reshape the windscreen to the correct armored "V" shape

Sounds straightforward, eh? There are probably several ways to go about each change, but here's what I did.

Rear fuselage. In 1/72 scale, the actuator fairings were easily removed with a grinding bit on a motor tool and careful sanding. I was worried that the removal process would cut through the thin plastic, so I reinforced the fairing area from inside each fuselage half with gap-filling super glue set with accelerator, **1**. As it turned out, I never broke through the plastic, but it is likely that you will if you are building a larger-scale kit. Photo **2** shows a fuselage half with the fairing removed and one unmodified.

Next I sanded the rear fuselage smooth and rescribed the paned detail. Since I planned to apply a natural metal finish, the surface had to be flawless.

Swapping wings. For this conversion I used the out-of-production Puget Sound Scale Models resin slatted wing designed for the Hasegawa F-86D Sabre Dog—the same wing was used on the A and E Sabres. (See sources for a substitute.) Since it was designed to fit a different kit, I had to make some modifications. The lower fuselage section of the resin wing was deeper than the Fujimi kit. I had to combine the bottom fuselage section of the Fujimi wing set with the resin wings. Some quick action with a razor saw produced all the parts I needed, **3**.

Since there were no longer any tabs and slots in the assembly, the wing/fuselage joint was potentially fragile. I merged the pieces with gap-filling super glue—this provided strength and filled the wing/fuselage seams. Remember, sand super glue

5

Paul scored clear PETG plastic for the new windscreen.

6

The oversize strip is easy to bend once it has been scored.

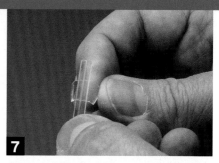

7

Once cut to size, the new V-shaped strip is glued to the kit windscreen.

right after it sets. As it cures, it hardens, making it harder than plastic and more difficult to sand.

I attached the new wings so that the landing gear bays lined up with those in the fuselage section. The position of the trailing edges of the wings should be the same as on the original. Since the new wing was narrower in chord than the kit wing, a stub of wing root at the leading edge remained on each side of the fuse-

lage, **4**. I carefully filed and sanded the stubs away.

Make sure the wings align properly. From the front, Sabre wings have about three degrees of dihedral, and without tabs or slots, the alignment is tricky. I used just a drop or two of gap-filling super glue near the trailing edge, then eyeballed each wing from the side, front, top, and bottom. Once a wing was in the correct position, I applied more super glue along the

seam by transferring small amounts with a toothpick. Then I set the glue with accelerator and immediately sanded the seams smooth.

The leading-edge slat tracks molded onto the resin wing were not cast well, so I cut them off and replaced them with styrene strip. The slats were molded separately. On real Sabres, leading-edge slats are deployed (extended) when the aircraft is at rest or at low airspeeds. Aerodynamic forces (increased speed or "Gs") retract these slats automatically. Some photos show parked Sabres with the slats retracted, but these were probably pinned in place for photographic or maintenance purposes. So if you want to model a slatted Sabre on the ground, you should deploy the slats.

Windscreen. The A model Sabres and many of the early E models had a V-shaped armored windscreen. I thought about carving a master for the new windscreen and vacuum- or stretch-forming copies, but I decided to do something that's a lot simpler and almost as good. I used the kit windscreen as a basis and added a clear plastic V plate to the front. After it was glued, sanded, polished, and the frames painted, you can barely tell that it is a composite.

First I cut a piece of .020" PETG clear sheet (available in plastic supply stores) into a 3"-long, $\frac{3}{8}$"-wide strip. Next, I scored a groove down the center of the strip with a sharp blade, **5**. I scored the line twice, once with the blade angled slightly to one side, the next with the blade angled to the other side. This produced a V-shaped groove about halfway through the

Sabre variants

The changes made to the Sabre during its production run were incremental, and all were done to enhance the jet's already stellar performance. Improvements were made to increase the thrust of the J47 jet engine and improved gunsights, but the real advances came with the "all-flying" tailplanes first seen on the F-86E. These had hinged elevators as usual, but the entire horizontal stabilizer moved as well to increase maneuverability. The rear fuselage of the Sabre was reshaped slightly to cover the actuators for the new tailplanes. This produced a pronounced fairing ahead of the tailplanes. During the F-86E production run, the windscreen was redesigned with a flat armored front panel.

During the production run of the F-86F-25 and F-30, designers came up with a new wing to improve high-speed maneuverability. It replaced the original wing leading-edge slats with an extension that increased wing chord. This extension was six inches wide at the wing root, tapering to three inches wide at the wing tip, so it also increased the

wing-sweep angle. This was called the "6-3 wing" or "hard" wing, and featured a small fence on the upper surface of the leading edge. Modification "6-3 kits" were also produced, rushed to Korea, and installed on earlier F-86F's and some Es.

The F-86F-40, made for the Japanese Self Defense Force, had a further improvement to the wing. This kept the increased chord of the 6-3 wing, but also reinstituted the leading-edge slats to improve low-speed handling. The F-40 wing also featured extended wing tips (one foot each), and this wing was also retrofitted to earlier USAF Sabres after the Korean War.

The improved and enlarged F-86H Sabre also went through wing changes during its production. Photos show most of them fitted with the F-40 wing, but some were built with the 6-3 "hard" leading edge with the small fence.

F-86D Dog Sabres had the early narrow-chord slatted wing, but the improved F-86L carried the F-40 wing.

- Paul Boyer

8 The new V-shaped windscreen before finishing.

9 Gap-filling super glue, careful sanding, and an overcoat of Future floor polish finishes the new windscreen.

10 Here's the model right after painting, but before decaling. Paul used strips of black decal sheet for the identification stripes.

11 Note the smoothly faired aft fuselage section typical of A-model Sabres.

plastic and allowed the plastic to be folded easily, **6**. The strip was much wider than needed on the windscreen, but the extra width made it easier to fold. It was also much longer than I needed, allowing me to cut it to the right shape later. The fold ended up being about a 120-degree angle.

With the score folded, the next job was to cut down the width of the strip. I measured the width of the kit's flat windscreen panel, divided that measurement by two, then used that figure for the width on either side of the fold. A couple of passes with a sharp blade cut the excess away from each side. Now the V-shaped strip was as wide as the flat panel, **7**.

The strip was next placed onto a sheet of 400-grit sandpaper with the V fold pointing up. With gentle sanding, the edges were beveled so it would fit snug to the flat windscreen.

The next step was to glue the new windscreen on top of the old. Plastic cement would frost the kit canopy

and would have little effect on the PETG strip, so I decided to use gap-filling super glue. This can also frost clear plastic, but a coat of Future floor polish on the clear plastic reduces this risk. Wait for the Future to cure—about 48 hours—before continuing.

I first glued the kit windscreen to the assembled fuselage, then sanded the small rectangular protrusion from the front of the kit's windscreen pedestal. I next sanded one end of the V-shaped strip so that it would fit flush on the nose at the bottom of the pedestal, then cut the other end a little longer than was needed to reach the top of the windscreen. With the strip carefully positioned, I placed a small drop of gap-filling super glue on each edge, allowing it to flow along the seam. An application of accelerator set the strip in place. Now I had to sand down the top end and bridge the small opening at the top with sheet styrene, **8**.

Now the windscreen has the right shape, but the seams were still visi-

ble—so I sanded carefully using fine, extra-fine, and polishing sticks to smooth out the seams. Next I gave it a dose of Novus 2 plastic polish, all the while being careful not to apply too much pressure and break the fragile plastic. Finally, I brushed on another coat of Future and placed the fuselage aside for another 48 hours, **9**.

Simple Sabre. The early Sabres were overall natural metal, with a few panels noticeably darker and some painted fiberglass. Early A models had fiberglass intakes that were either painted or left in a natural brown color. The aircraft I chose to model, the one flown by Capt. James Jabara on his "ace" mission (see p. 62) was a late F-86A-5 with an aluminum intake with its small dark gray cover of the radar ranging gunsight at the top.

After masking the V-shaped windscreen and covering the cockpit, I airbrushed the model with SnJ Spray Metal. Most of these combat Sabres were pretty weathered, so I didn't polish the finish. I tinted more SnJ with a little Testor gloss black to

Early Sabres had automatic leading-edge slats on narrow chord wings. The horizontal stabilizers were conventional (not "all-flying" as in later models).

Paul mounted a helmet on top of the windscreen. He cut the head off of a pilot figure and hollowed it out with a dental bit in a motor tool.

paint some of the wing and fuselage panel, then added still more black for the gun panel and exhaust area.

The first combat Sabres had black and white identification. stripes on the fuselage and wingtips, and a narrow black stripe up the vertical tail. Jabara's ace Sabre had no special markings—no nose art, no kill marks, not even crew names on the canopy. After allowing the metallic finish to cure, I masked and airbrushed a wide white area on the fuselage and wingtips, **10** and **11**. When that was dry, I added black decal stripes cut to approximately eight scale inches wide.

I went through my Sabre decal collection and cut the proper digits out for the FU-319 "buzz number" on the rear fuselage. I created the tail markings on computer and laser-printed them onto clear decal sheet. Insignias and USAF for the wings came from Sabre sheets as well.

The main gear struts from the Fujimi kit weren't an exact fit for the new wing, but with a little filing and a drop of super glue, the struts were firmly attached. Since I wanted this model in the "at rest" pose, I opened the wheel covers (which open as hydraulic pressure bleeds off after engine shutdown). The interiors of the wells were painted yellow zinc chromate, but the inside of the doors were aluminum. I left the speed brakes closed.

I hope you have learned some helpful kitbashing techniques. At least you've learned you don't have to settle for yet another F-86F!

Capt. James Jabara's Sabre

On May 20, 1951, Capt. James Jabara achieved "first jet ace" status by gaining his fifth and sixth MiG-15 kills. By this time, Jim's original unit, the 334th Fighter Interceptor Squadron, had rotated back to Japan, but Jim remained behind to fly the remainder of his 125 missions and try to achieve his fifth victory.

On the day of the historical mission, Jabara was unable to drop his right wing tank. Pilots experiencing this malfunction were supposed to return to base, but the fight was already on, so Jabara engaged with the stubborn tank hanging on the wing. Jabara proceeded to shoot down two MiG-15 jets and safely returned to base.

There has been much misinformation about Jabara's "ace" Sabre. When Jabara landed on K-13 (Suwon Air Base) there were no regular public relations photographers to record the event, but General Electric technical representatives Irv Clark and Leo Fournier were there; they took several photos, showing the still-hung drop tank.

Here's where the confusion begins. The next day, May 21, the 5th Air Force gathered all the photographers together to re-enact the landing. However, Jim's "ace" Sabre (49-1319) was not available, having been taken to maintenance to remove the hung drop tank and to have other repairs. So the 5th Air Force staged the event with Jabara being hoisted on fellow pilots' shoulders and being carried away from a different Sabre (49-1210). If this weren't confusing enough, the entire scene was re-enacted again in the afternoon, this time using Sabre 49-1318!

After this mission, Jabara was hustled back to Japan so that his "jet ace" status could be used for publicity purposes. Jabara eventually returned to combat, flying later-model Sabres and ending the war with 15 MiG kills, only one behind Joseph McConnell. Jabara was killed in an automobile accident in 1966.

– Larry Davis

Detailing a 1/48 scale MiG-17

A LITTLE EXTRA TIME AND PHOTOETCHED PARTS WILL TURN THE SMER/AIRFIX KIT INTO A STANDOUT MODEL

Jiri Lizler built his Smer MiG-17 out of the box using the alternate parts to model a Lim-6 bis in Polish service. Note the prominent drag-chute housing under the rudder. Jan Vlasak photo.

Smer's 1/48 scale MiG-17 is a breakthrough for this small Czech kit manufacturer. After years of reissuing old Heller and Artiplast/Merit/Aurora kits dating back to the late 1950s, Smer has produced its own mold for this new kit. Incidentally, Smer's MiG has been repackaged by Airfix, a major player in the European hobby industry, so the kit is easier to find in the United States and Canada.

By Jiri Lizler

Smer's kit represents the MiG-17F Fresco C, the most numerous of the many versions of this famous fighter. The kit also provides alternate parts for the Lim-6 bis, the Polish-built version of the MiG-17F with its characteristic drag-chute housing beneath the rudder. Also included are special weapons and pylons for the Egyptian-modified MiGs that saw combat action in the Six-Day War against Israel.

Brassy additions. I built my model out of the box without superdetailing, but you may want to improve your MiG. There's room for improvement over Smer's generally good detail and accuracy. Adding Eduard's photoetched brass detail set is an easy way to improve the model. The set includes relief-etched instrument panel and consoles (with photographic film reproductions of the gauges), ejection seat details, landing gear tie-down rings, wheel hub details, and an afterburner flame holder.

Improvements step-by-step. Let's start accurizing and detailing at the nose and work back to the tail.

The Eduard photoetched brass detail set includes a photographic film of the gauges for the instrument panel.

Remove the hump on the top of the nose; this was an early antenna fairing, not characteristic of most MiG-17Fs. Many Frescos had a bar-shaped SRD-1M rangefinder antenna in this position. You can make this with stretched sprue. Add a tiny stretched-sprue landing gear position indicator post forward and to the left of the windscreen. Add the aftermarket photoetched cockpit and seat details according to the Eduard instructions.

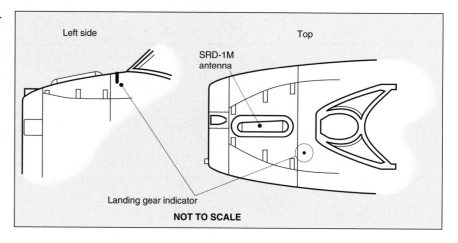

The three fences on each wing should extend to the leading edge. This isn't an easy fix, but if you can't live with this inaccuracy, try fairing in a chunk of .020" sheet styrene to the front of each fence.

Add stretched-sprue landing gear indicator posts to the top of each wing.

Smer's main landing gear struts are OK, but you could add the tie-down rings from the Eduard photoetched set. Hub detail from Eduard also helps the main and nose gear wheels. Add stretched-sprue brake lines to the main gear struts and bays following the photos.

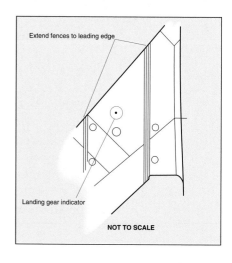

A look into the left main gear bay reveals wing structure, hydraulic plumbing, and electrical wiring. Here's a look at the left main landing gear of a real MiG-17. Note the hydraulic brake line along the strut.

SOURCE
Eduard photoetched detail sets: Military Model Distributors, 1115 Crowley Drive, Carrollton, TX 75011-5010, (214) 242-8663

REFERENCES
OKB MiG, A History of the Design Bureau and Its Aircraft Piotr Butowski and Jay Miller, Aerofax Inc. for Specialty Press, Stillwater, Minnesota, 1991
Random Thoughts J. Hornat, articles in (IPMS/Canada) Nos. 5 and 8, 1975
MiG-17 in Detail & Scale B. Slatton, Detail & Scale Publications, El Paso, Texas, 1978
MiG-17 Fresco in Action Hans-Heiri Stapfer, Squadron/Signal Publications, Carrollton , Texas,1962

Moving to the tail, insert the photoetched flame holder inside the after burner tube according to the Eduard instructions.

There are a few inaccuracies in the shape and details of the aft end of the Smer MiG. The tiny rod projecting from the trailing edge of the vertical fin is the right shape and size for the Syrene 2 tail-warning radar antenna, but it is placed too high between the two-section rudder. Carefully shave it off and place it farther down, then add a stretched-sprue position light above it.

The outline of the speed brakes is incorrect. The problem is the bottom edge is too low. The drawing shows the proper shape. When the MiG-17 is at rest, the speed brakes are usually cracked open a few degrees. Superdetailers may want to cut open the brakes and add interior detail. The forward section of the speed brake well exposes the exhaust pipe while the aft end of the well is covered with sheet metal to fair in with the fuselage.

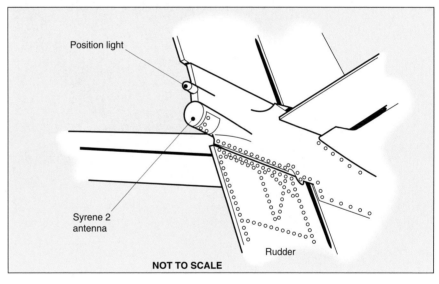

Position light

Syrene 2 antenna

Rudder

NOT TO SCALE

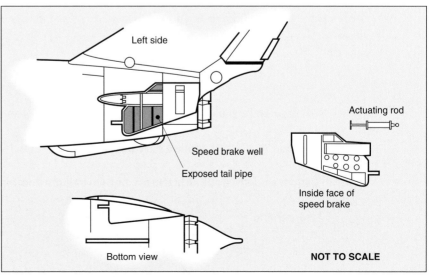

Left side

Actuating rod

Speed brake well

Exposed tail pipe

Inside face of speed brake

Bottom view

NOT TO SCALE

CHAPTER FIFTEEN

Easy Camouflage with "soft" masks

NOT GOOD AT SPRAYING FINE LINES? TRY THIS SHORTCUT

If you can't get your airbrush to spray fine lines, try "soft masking" your next camouflage scheme. Paul's 1/48 scale Tamiya A-1H Skyraider wears the Tactical scheme used in Vietnam in the late 1960s.

Do you envy those modelers who can apply feathered multicolored camouflage to aircraft models? I sure do. I keep practicing with my airbrush (and trying different airbrushes), but I'm seldom comfortable enough to try it freehand.

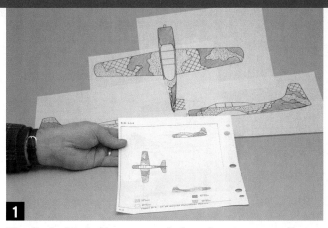

1

The first step in the process is to enlarge a camouflage pattern drawing to the scale of the model with a variable enlarging/reducing copy machine.

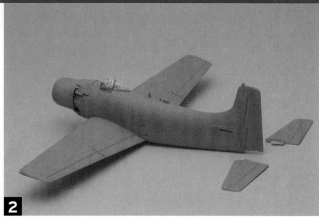

2

The entire top of the Skyraider was painted FS 30219 tan, the lightest of the three top colors.

By Paul Boyer
Photos by William Zuback
and Jim Forbes

Scale overspray. Most full-size machines are spray-painted without masks by a crew with industrial sprayers. The guidelines for the camouflage patterns are simple diagrams in technical manuals. In this real-world scenario, the demarcation lines between colors are not sharp—the edges of the colors are soft, caused by the slight overspray of the paint coming out of the spray gun.

In the scale modeling world, I have to balance paint/thinner ratios, adjust paint volume, tweak air pressure, and maintain just the right distance between the airbrush nozzle and the model. It's enough to drive me sane.

One method that works for me is using "soft" masks. What are soft masks, and where do they come from? Soft masks are cut from stiff paper or light cardboard and attached to the model so that the edges hover slightly above the surface. This allows just a tiny bit of overspray along the color's edge to soften the line, looking much like the hand-sprayed camouflage of the real thing.

I detect a pattern here . . . To create masks (hard or soft), refer to a pattern. Usually, a model's instruction sheet shows the pattern for the paint scheme. If not, check reference books or official government tech orders if you can obtain them.

3

The tan areas of the camouflage scheme were cut out of the drawings and traced onto manila-folder paper. The stiffness of this paper holds up well against the force of the spray.

4

The sticky putty is rolled and warmed, then pulled into a thin "worm." The worm is then applied about ¼" inside the edge on the underside of the cardboard pattern.

Sticky putties

Sticky putty comes in many brands and colors, and can be found in hardware stores and home centers. Another common one is Blue Tac, found in craft stores.

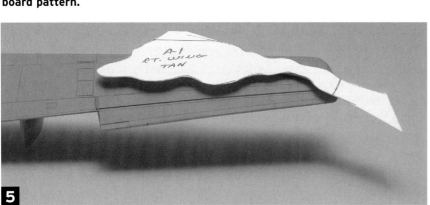

5

The sticky putty worm holds the cardboard pattern about ⅛" off the surface, essential to create the soft, feathered effect.

6

All the cardboard patterns to mask the tan areas are applied. The model is now ready to have the light green sprayed on.

My example here is the 1/48 scale Tamiya A-1 painted in the U.S. Air Force "Tactical" paint scheme of tan, medium green, dark green, and light gray. The diagram I used was from an old copy of the USAF Technical Order 1-1-4. I had to enlarge the camouflage pattern to the same scale as the model. This isn't hard if you have access to a copier that can reduce and enlarge. Figuring the enlargement is a little tricky, so grab a calculator and a ruler.

Measure the model you are about to paint. In my case, the 1/48 scale Skyraider's span was 12½". The span of the diagram was a little over 3". To figure the enlargement size, divide what you need (the size of the model) by what you have (the size of the drawing). In this case, the result was approximately 4, which translated to 400 percent (4 times as big). Now, set the enlarging copier to 400 percent and shoot. If your copier can't enlarge more than 200 percent, you may need to enlarge the first enlargement! Check the resulting copy with the model to be sure it's the right size, **1**.

First color. Now is a good time to

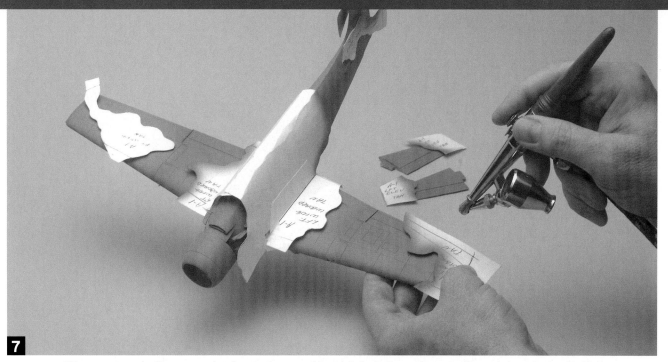

7

When you apply the second color, make sure the airbrush doesn't spray the paint underneath the masks. Spray at 90 degrees or slightly away from the edges.

paint the model overall with the lightest color of the camouflage. Generally, it is a good idea to paint the lightest color first, since it's easier to cover light colors with dark. No masks were needed here, except to cover the cockpit interior. I airbrushed my Skyraider's top overall tan (FS 30219), **2**. While the bottom color (FS 36622) is even lighter, I decided to paint the bottom last (more on that later).

Since copier paper is rather flimsy, you'll need to transfer the pattern onto heavy paper or light cardboard for the masks. If you have a copier that can print on light card stock, you can skip this next step.

Determine which areas on the camouflage drawing represent the color you have already painted on the model. In this case, the spotted areas represent tan. Cut out all the "tan" segments from the drawings, and trace each one onto light card stock—I used manila folders, **3**. Now cut them out and label them; for example, "A-1 right wing outboard tan." While you are in the cutting mood, repeat the procedure for the next darker color, in this case, the

8

After the second color is dry, the next set of masks is applied, leaving uncovered the areas to be sprayed in the last color.

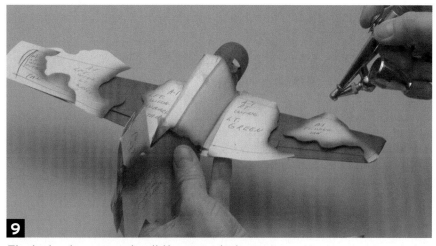

9

The last color goes onto all the unmasked areas.

10

Removing the masks reveals the tri-color camouflage scheme. Note the tightly feathered color demarcation lines.

lighter of the two greens, FS 34102.

Sticky stencils. What you have at this point are light cardboard masks that will cover areas on the model. There are several ways to attach the masks to the model for painting, but I use sticky putty, available in craft and hardware stores. Roll a large piece of the putty between your hands until it's soft. After rolling it into a long thin "worm," cut off pieces and stick them onto the back of the cardboard masks, **4.** Place the putty at least ¼" in from the edges.

Now you can position the masks for the tan areas on the model by pressing them gently in place. If you goof, you can peel the masks off and reposition them easily. The cardboard should stand out from the model surface by about ⅛", **5.** Position all the masks for the tan areas. You may have to curl and shape the cardboard to allow it to go over curved surfaces, **6.**

Second color. Prepare your next color (the next darker one, in my case FS 34102 green), and load the airbrush. If you can, drop the air pressure down to about 10 psi to reduce overspray and adjust the air-

brush tip so that you can paint a line about ⅛"wide. Spray along the masked edge first, **7.** Angle the airbrush so that you are spraying perpendicular (90 degrees) to the mask or away from the mask—never towards it. After you have painted around the masks, fill in the rest of the exposed areas.

Make sure you have sprayed all the areas that need to be painted in the second color. Wait for the paint to dry 24 hours, then add the masks that will cover the second color, **8,** and spray on the third color, **9.** Follow this procedure for all the remaining colors. You don't need to make masks for the last color, because (usually) there are no more colors to be sprayed on.

Carefully peel off the masks and you should have a beautifully airbrushed camouflage job, **10.** Keep the masks (remove the putty, though!), as you can use them again if you build another model of the same camouflaged subject.

The Skyraider project had an interesting twist. The bottom color (FS 36622 Light Gray) followed a rela-

Precut "hard" masks

Some camouflage schemes, such as those applied to British aircraft in World War II, were masked with rubber mats, creating sharp color demarcation lines. You can cut masks for schemes such as these from masking tape, or you can purchase pre-cut adhesive masks from the sources below:

Black Magic Meteor Productions, P.O. Box 3956, Merrifield, VA 22116, 703-971-0500, www.eCompuQuest.com/meteor/ enter.html

Express Masks Eduard Model Accessories, Obrince 170, 43521 Obrince, Czech Republic, www.eduard.cz/frame_info.htm

11

Cellophane tape, held off the surface by the curve of the cowl, is used as a mask when painting the underside color.

tively straight line along the cowl, and the sharp corners of the rear fuselage helped define the demarcation line. Instead of painting the bottom first, and trying to cut and match the masks for the three top side colors, I decided to make life easier and apply the bottom color last. I even used tape here, allowing the curve of the cowl to hold the tape above the demarcation line, **11**.

Touchup. The soft mask system is not perfect. If you use too much air pressure or too much paint volume, overspray can creep too far underneath the edges of the masks, "bounce" against the putty, and settle on the model. It looks much like a subtle shadow, **12**. You may choose to go back over the area with the previous color and "retouch" the problem, or you could try sanding away the offending overspray with an extra-fine sanding stick. Go lightly and slowly to avoid sanding through the underlying color.

For modelers who have figured out all the nuances of their particular airbrush setup, this method may seem

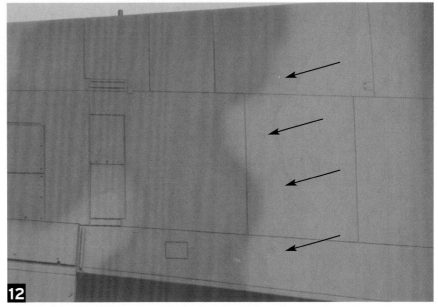

12

If too much paint is applied, or if too much air pressure is used, you might get a shadow underneath the mask. This can be touched up or carefully sanded away.

like unnecessary work. However for those of us who are still mystified by the miracle tool, soft masking camouflage will help flatten out that steep learning curve.

CHAPTER SIXTEEN

Building an F-100C Super Sabre

BACKDATING MONOGRAM'S F-100D

Making an F-100C from Monogram's 1/48 scale D model isn't difficult and offers modelers a wide variety of colorful paint schemes. Ben Brown will show you how he converted it.

I remember the day, some 40 years ago, when the Thunderbirds flew their fabulous arrival show at McConnell Air Force Base, Kansas, preparing for their full-up air show. They flew so low that I felt I could reach up and touch the silvery F-100s as they flashed overhead. Since then the F-100 has been a favorite modeling subject for me.

By Ben Brown

Monogram's 1/48 scale F-100D is by far the best available Super Sabre kit. Unfortunately, the only way you can get an earlier version than the D is to do some cutting.

Paul Boyer's conversion of an Esci 1/72 scale F-100D to a C in his book *Building and Displaying Scale Aircraft Models* (Kalmbach) inspired me to try his techniques on the bigger Monogram kit. Backdating the Monogram kit isn't hard, and the larger scale lets you include changes that aren't as noticeable in 1/72 scale. The late F-100A and F-100C were externally almost identical, so I will point out some of the subtle differences between the two. I found it easier to make many of the necessary modifications before assembling the kit.

Wings. The F-100A and C had no trailing-edge flaps on the wings. These were added to the D model and are identifiable by the kink in the trailing edge line. After gluing the wing parts together, cut the inboard part of the kit flaps off so the wings have straight trailing edges, **1**. Fill the kit's flap and aileron hinge lines for later rescribing.

Sand the trailing edges of the wings to get thin edges. While you're sanding, remove the reinforcing straps molded into the underside of the wings.

If you are building an F-100A, fill the slot for the in-flight refueling probe, remove the box-shaped bulge aft of the refueling probe slot, and fill the outer pylon holes. The F-100C initially was fitted with a straight in-flight refueling probe but this was later changed to the bent probe. Fortunately, Monogram provides both types, so you can choose the one you need.

I used 1/48 scale drawings from Bert Kinzey's *F-100 Super Sabre in Detail & Scale* as a reference for the wing panel lines. The drawings don't quite match the kit wing, so I adapted the panel lines to fit, **2**. Don't

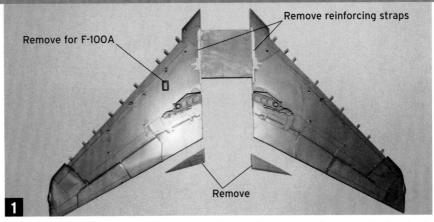

1 Remove reinforcing straps / Remove for F-100A / Remove

One of two major changes from the D to the C was the wing. The C wing had no flaps, so the Monogram D wings must be modified.

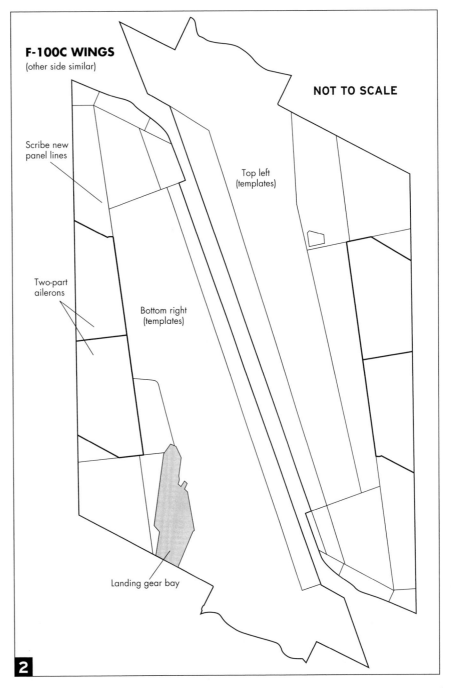

2 **F-100C WINGS** (other side similar) / NOT TO SCALE / Scribe new panel lines / Top left (templates) / Two-part ailerons / Bottom right (templates) / Landing gear bay

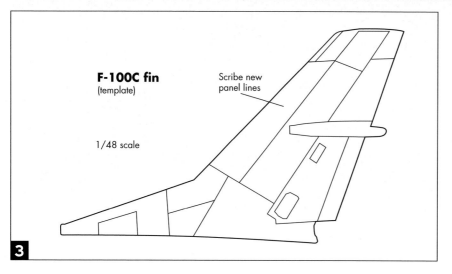

F-100C fin
(template)

Scribe new panel lines

1/48 scale

3

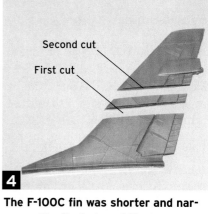

Second cut

First cut

4

The F-100C fin was shorter and narrower. The first step of the conversion is to take ¼" from the kit's fin.

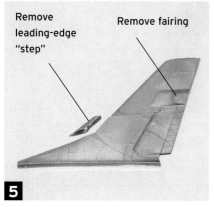

Remove leading-edge "step"

Remove fairing

5

Reuniting the base of the fin and the tip provides the correct height.

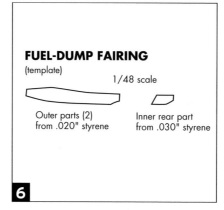

FUEL-DUMP FAIRING
(template)

1/48 scale

Outer parts (2) from .020" styrene

Inner rear part from .030" styrene

6

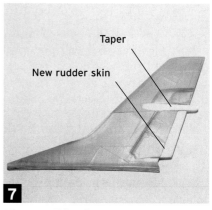

Taper

New rudder skin

7

More modifications are necessary for the C model fin. Sheet styrene makes the new fuel-dump fairing and smooth rudder.

install the wing fences (part No. 75), as they were not fitted to the C model. During final assembly, add a static dissipator wick to each wingtip, approximately ¼" from the tip. Each can be made with short section of wire.

Tail. The vertical stabilizer on the F-100D was taller, broader, and had a different fairing over the fuel vent than the C model, **3**. The D rudder was also longer. The following surgery converts the D fin to the C version. First, glue the fin halves together. Measure ⅞" from the bottom of the rudder and mark a line parallel to the bottom of the rudder. Cut the fin along this line, **4**. Measure at least twice, so you don't cut your fin too short (as I did, the first time). Now remove a ¼"

section from the bottom of the upper fin piece.

Cut the rear of the fuel-vent fairing off so it is flush with the trailing edge of the fin, and fill the hole with gap-filling super glue. This will make removing the rest of the fairing much easier, and the crater left by the fairing will already be filled. File the fuel-vent fairing away, and then glue the upper and lower sections of the fin together, making sure the trailing edges line up. Cut away the step in the lower leading edge, fill gaps along the seams, and sand the seams and leading edge smooth, **5**.

Add the fuel-vent fairing parts using the template provided, **6**. Cut the two outer surfaces from .020" sheet styrene and the rear core from .030". The outer pieces are glued to

the sides of the fin just above the rudder, and the inner piece fits between them aft of the trailing edge.

Once the glue has set, file and sand the fairing so it is of constant width along its entire length but still protrudes slightly from the surface of the fin. The bottom edge of the fairing is gently curved, **7**. Seen from behind, the top of the fairing is rounded, while the bottom is flat.

There are two lights at the end of the fairing, orange on top of clear, **8**. The fuel vent is a tube that protrudes downward from the bottom of the fairing. Make the lights and vent from stretched sprue. Use a ¹⁄₃₂" wide sliver of .005" styrene sheet to simulate the sheet-metal mount for the static dissipator wick. The wick can be made from wire.

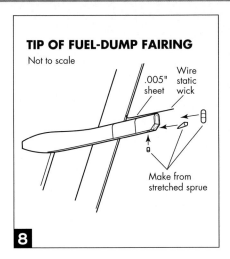

TIP OF FUEL-DUMP FAIRING

Not to scale

.005" sheet

Wire static wick

Make from stretched sprue

8

9

An Eduard photoetched brass instrument panel graces the cockpit of Ben's F-100C.

10

Behind the seat is a canopy defogger made from stretched sprue.

11

RHAW boxes (painted white) weren't fitted to the F-100C, so carve them away.

12

The speed brake of the F-100C was narrower. White-painted areas are to be cut away.

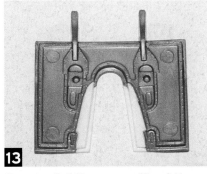

13

Ben created the new profile of the C-model speed brake with two layers of sheet styrene.

Some early F-100s did not have the rudder with the exposed ribs. The particular jet I modeled had a smooth rudder, so I skinned it with .010" styrene sheet. Although I didn't, you should fill and sand the center hinge tab on each side of the rudder.

Rescribe the panel lines lost in sanding. Again, the drawings in *Detail & Scale* didn't quite match the kit parts, so I engraved them as in drawing 3.

Cockpit and upper fuselage. The main difference between the F-100C and D cockpits is the instrument panel. Fortunately, Eduard's F-100D detail set (No. 48-183) also includes an F-100C instrument panel, **9**, so no alteration is necessary. The F-100A panel is similar to the C panel.

I added a throttle made from stretched sprue, and used the Eduard landing gear handle, rudder pedals, and circuit breaker panels. I used a white metal seat from Aeroclub (No. ABEJ413) because the kit seat has the parachute pack molded into the seatback. The pack usually was not left in the jet unless the aircraft was on alert.

The F-100A and C had a different configuration from the D on the deck behind the seat. Remove the pyramid shape from kit part 16. Cover the hole with .010" sheet styrene, and then add the canopy defogging ducts, **10**. They can be made from wire or stretched sprue. Make the two cylinders from the kit sprue.

Remove the boxes above the instrument panel marked in white, **11**. They are part of the Radar

REFERENCES
F-100 Super Sabre in Detail & Scale Bert Kinzey, TAB Books, Blue Ridge Summit, Pennsylvania, 1989
Colors & Markings of the F-100 Super Sabre David W. Menard, TAB Books, Blue Ridge Summit, Pennsylvania, 1990
North American F-100 Super Sabre (Osprey Air Combat) David Anderton, Osprey Publishing Limited, London, England, 1987
Aviation Nut Webzine http://hometown.aol.com/svanaken/index.htm. A photo of this airplane is at geocities.com/capecanaveral/hangar/2118/acft/airfr.html

SOURCES
Ejection seat Aeroclub 5 Silverwood Avenue, Ravenhead, Nottingham NG15 9BU, England
Cockpit details Eduard Model Accessories, 435 21 Obrnice 170, Czech Republic, www.eduard.cz
Sheet styrene Plastruct, 1020 S. Wallace Place, City of Industry, CA 91748, www.plastruct.com
Panel scriber Bare-metal Foil Co., P.O. Box 82, Farmington, MI 48332, 248-476-4366, www.bare-metal.com
SnJ Spray Metal SnJ Model Products, P.O. Box 292713, Sacramento, CA 95829, 916-428-7217

14

The C wheel covers were not as complicated as the D-model's covers. Black wires replicate hydraulic lines to the cover locks.

15

Monogram's afterburner nozzle is a bit restricted. Ben bored it out and deepened it with a roll of sheet styrene.

PROJECT AT A GLANCE
  This project involves converting Monogram's 1/48 scale F-100D (current kit No. 85-5496) into an earlier F-100C, and adding details to the model. Modelers should have some experience with "plastic surgery" and smoothing the modified parts for a natural-metal finish. You'll also need:
  • sharp hobby knife
  • razor saw
  • plastic scribing tool
  • filler putty
  • sandpaper
  • Eduard detail set (No. 48-183)
  • Aeroclub ejection seat (No. ABEJ413)
  • .005", .010", .020", .030" sheet styrene

EARLY F-100 NOSE WHEELS

1/48 scale

F-100C nose wheel   F-100A nose wheel

If you model an early F-100, look for wheels such as these in your spares box to replace the kit nose wheels. You can also make new hubs from sheet styrene.

16

KIT OUTER WING PYLON

Side view   (templates)

← Forward   Extend with sheet styrene
Top view

1/48 scale

450-GALLON FUEL TANKS

Tail end of Monogram F-101B Voodoo tank

.020" sheet styrene fins

17

Homing and Warning System on the D. While you have the upper fuselage in hand, remove the stabilators. This will make cleaning up the joints between the upper and lower fuselage halves and the tail cone much easier. Fill the little hole on the spine where the D model's rectangular antenna is supposed to go.

Lower fuselage. The F-100D could carry a center-line store, and its ventral speed brake had a larger cutout to keep it from colliding with the store. The speed brake of the A and C had a narrower cutout. To make the kit's speed brake accurate for the C model, you'll have to modify both the speed brake and the bay in the bottom of the fuselage. The bay can be modified by filing away the areas I painted white, **12**.

Backdate the speed brake by using .020" sheet styrene to fill the cutouts and give them a straight edge, **13**. I used a second layer of .020" to add a

little extra detail on the inside of the speed brake. Fill the seam on the exterior with super glue and sand.

F-100s were fitted with arrestor hooks between 1960 and 1961. Fill the holes for the arrestor hook if your model depicts an earlier jet.

The large inboard wheel covers on the F-100D did not swing through a 90-degree arc when opened because of the provision for the centerline store. They each had an extra panel that opened to allow the main wheel to clear the cover. Earlier versions of the D and all F-100A and C models had one-piece covers, which hung vertically when opened. Monogram has molded the covers and the center bracket from which they hang as one piece.

To backdate the wheel covers, I first separated the covers from the center bracket, then glued the small panels to the covers. Next I removed all of the detail inside the covers. I

made a new inside panel using .010" sheet vacuum-formed over a wood master to obtain the D-shaped dent which made space for the brakes protruding from the wheels, **14**. I added styrene-strip spacers between the covers and new inner panels. Each cover had two hydraulic lines that actuated the cover locks. I made them from wire.

Tailcone. Early F-100s had an iris-type exhaust, so use part 5 for the F-100C, **15**. (The F-102-type exhaust also provided in the kit was used only on Air National Guard F-100D's and F's.) I opened up the exhaust with a motor tool and deepened it with a roll of sheet styrene and a J-57 turbine from the Monogram F-101 kit (No. 85-5843). I used Eduard's photoetched brass afterburner ring.

Nose gear wheels. Later in its service life, the F-100C used the same nose wheels as the D. Earlier F-100s had a spoked wheel hub or a hub with six holes in it, **16**. I began making my six-holed hubs by fashioning "hubcaps" from styrene sheet, then gluing them in place. Then I drilled six 1/32" holes all the way through the wheel hubs. Getting the six holes evenly spaced around the hubs turned out to be the most difficult part of the project.

Drop tanks. F-100s were often seen with 450-gallon ferry tanks, which is what I hung on my model. I

"Charlie Huns"

The F-100C was the second production version of North American's Super Sabre. Pilots affectionately called it the "Hun," short for Hundred. The original A model, after early testing troubles (which killed famous test pilot George Welch), was the U.S. Air Force's entry into the supersonic era. While it was a good gun platform, the A model couldn't tote much in the way of ordnance and didn't hold enough fuel to feed the afterburning J-57 engine for long. A total of 202 A models were built.

North American designers developed the C model to fix these deficiencies. (The B model eventually became the F-107.) With a new wing and enlarged fuel tanks, the C model could carry a variety of external ordnance and fuel tanks. It was also equipped for in-flight refueling. The Air Force accepted 476 C models.

The "Charlie" model of the F-100 was the primary fighter bomber in the Tactical Air Command in the late 1950s, and it served in units in U.S. Air Forces in Europe (USAFE). Both the Thunderbirds and the Skyblazers (USAFE's demonstration team) flew C models (the T-Birds also flew D models). Many of the most colorful Super Sabres were C models.

By the time the Vietnam War heated up, most C models had been assigned to Reserve and Air National Guard units. Four ANG units flying C models were put on active duty and sent to Vietnam: Colorado, Iowa, New Mexico, and New York.

- Paul Boyer

thought these tanks looked like the 450-gallon drop tank used on the F-101 Voodoo. If you want them on your model, grab a pair from the Monogram F-101B and add fins cut from sheet styrene, **17.** For pylons, add a ¼" splice to the F-100 outboard pylons (kit parts No. 72) and lengthen the sway braces.

Finishing. Because so much raised detail was lost during modification, I rescribed the entire model. I used a scriber from Bare-Metal Foil and a flexible straightedge. Several light passes work better than trying to get the line perfect in one pass.

I painted my model using SnJ Spray Metal and Testor Metalizer paints. Both of these are buffable metallics. The toughness of the SnJ finish enabled me to mask and paint the blue squadron colors over the aluminum finish. The F-100C landing gear bays and speed-brake bay were usually painted green zinc chromate, but the inner faces of the gear doors and speed brake were usually natural metal.

The decals came from my spares box. My model depicts an F-100C from the 334th Fighter Day Squadron of the 4th Fighter Day Wing from Seymour Johnson Air Force Base, North Carolina, in 1958.

The Super Sabre had some of the most colorful squadron markings ever applied to U.S. fighters, and building an F-100C allows many more markings possibilities. Before the green and brown camouflage of the Vietnam War era, natural-metal F-100s were adorned with multicolored banners, chevrons, and stars. Skyblazers, anyone?

[Thanks to Scott Van Aken for photos and to Norm Filer for landing gear information.]

CHAPTER SEVENTEEN

BIG-SCALE F-4E Phantom II

A PROFESSIONAL MODELER SHARES HIS TRICKS FOR BUILDING A LARGE-SCALE KIT

Revell's 1/32 scale F-4E Phantom II is a big model, taking up nearly two feet of shelf space from nose to tail.

Bigger is better. You know, like Paul Bunyan and Shaquille O'Neal. Bigger

can be better with model aircraft, too, but large-scale projects pose mod-

eling challenges of their own. For example, although 1/72 scale instrument

panels can be dispatched quickly via a tiny decal, 1/32 scale "front offices"

demand more attention to detail—there's more room, and more to see.

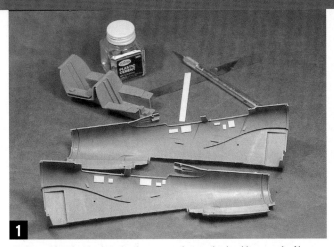

1. John attached sheet styrene placards to the cockpit walls to add detail.

2. To make it easier to pick out instrument panel details, apply a wash first. The wash accentuates the edges of each gauge.

3. The excess wash on the instrument panels and radar mount is removed with cotton swabs.

4. To get that glassy look, apply quick-setting clear epoxy to each gauge.

By John Adelmann
Photos by the author
and Jim Forbes

The Phantom is a large fighter, and its pilots often affectionately call it the "rhino," in part because of its big nose. I'll use Revell-Monogram's 1/32 scale F-4E Phantom II without aftermarket accessories to illustrate assembly, painting, washing, and weathering techniques for improving the appearance of large-scale aircraft models.

Inside out. Before any fuselage can be assembled, the cockpit interior must be completed. To jazz up the Phantom's interior, cut sheet styrene into small rectangles to replicate switch panels and glue them to the sidewalls, **1.** Don't overdo this—too many pieces look odd. After coating the interior parts and the inside of the fuselage with FS 36231 Dark Gull Gray, paint the styrene pieces flat black and dry-brush them chrome silver.

Now spruce up both instrument panels and consoles. Protect the gray-painted parts with several air-brushed coats of Future acrylic floor polish, every modeler's favorite household product.

When the Future is dry, wash the panels and tub with thinned gloss black water-based paint, **2.** This helps establish the position of every dial, faceplate, and crevice. I make my wash by mixing one to two parts of water-based gloss black paint to ten parts of water, then adding a drop or two of dishwashing liquid. The gloss paint rolls over the surface better than a flat paint, and the dishwashing liquid makes it easy to remove the dried excess wash with a slightly moistened cotton swab, **3.** The wash makes the dials stand out, and in some cases, they may not require any further painting.

Next, dry-brush the raised detail with chrome silver. If you cower in fear when selecting the details of any scale cockpit, applying a black wash first will put your mind at ease.

Now the fun begins. To add zip to the instrument faces, mix a little two-part clear epoxy and apply it to the dials with a sharp toothpick, **4.** This goo sets up quickly, so mix only as much as you can use in a few minutes. It's better to do just three or four dials at a time. When the epoxy begins to get stringy, it's time to quit.

5 Seat frames were painted charcoal black, then dry-brushed with chrome silver to accentuate the raised details.

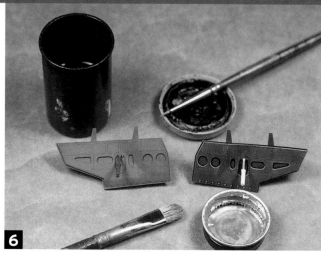

6 The red-painted speed brakes take on a new look (right) when dry-brushed, dipped in Future, and washed.

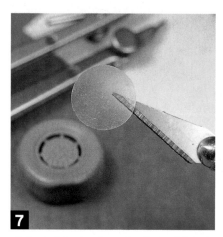

7 John cuts wheel masks from frisket film, measuring the diameter needed with a draftsman's compass.

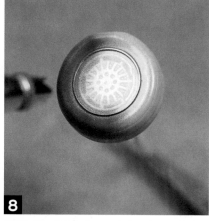

8 With the frisket mask in place, John sprays on the tire color.

If you don't mix the epoxy in proper proportions, the dial faces will remain tacky and attract dust. If this happens, you can carefully insert a knife blade into the center of the glob, pop the epoxy out, and start over. Another solution is to brush Future on the dial face to seal the epoxy. Future will also restore the shine on the dials if they accidentally receive clear flat overspray.

Instead of painting the ejection seat frames black, spray them flat charcoal black (a mix of dark gray and black), and then dry-brush with chrome silver to bring out the details, **5**. The afterburner grids and the engine intake knobs can be dry-brushed with chrome silver, too.

Seat cushions airbrushed with olive drab can be dry-brushed with FS 30277 Armor Sand, then glossed and later washed to accentuate the seatbelt-harness straps. After the wash dries and the excess is removed, paint the harnesses tan and the buckles silver.

Underwing things. Spray the underwing speed brakes' interior surfaces flat red, dry-brush them with chrome silver (dry-brushing works best on flat paint), and then apply several coats of Future before adding the wash. Future will also deepen the color—compare the left speed brake with the glossed one on the right, **6**. Repeat this process on the white-painted landing gear struts.

Big models usually have big wheels, and they have to be done right. I use two methods to paint the wheels. I shoot the nose wheels with flat white paint, gloss them with Future, then apply a wash. The wash accentuates the wheel's rim and makes it easier to paint the tire color. With the wheel impaled on a toothpick, I hold the paintbrush stationary and spin the wheel as the charcoal black paint flows on. For the larger main wheels, I paint the wheels as above, but then cut masks from frisket paper using a draftsman's compass, **7**. Then I airbrush the tire color, **8**.

Bigger is longer, too. The larger the model, the longer the seams. Rather than spend hours with increasingly finer grades of sandpaper to eliminate them, I use a specially designed seam scraper available from Micro-Mark, **9**. It has three sharp blades, each of which literally scrapes the excess plastic away. The trick here is to begin scraping about ¼" from either side of the seam, almost like peeling a carrot. This prevents flat spots, particularly noticeable on fuel tanks and fuselage spines. When the shiny glue residue disappears, you've gone far enough. A light sanding with 1800-grit sandpaper backed with a rubber block polishes the seams, **10**.

All the glued seams (even if they didn't need to be filled) should be polished smooth. Any roughness will

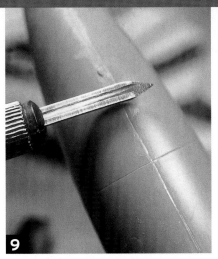

9 Micro-Mark's seam scraper is ideal for curved surfaces such as this drop tank's.

10 Final sanding is done with super-fine grit wet-or-dry sandpaper.

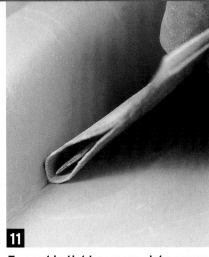

11 To sand in tight corners, John wraps sandpaper around a thin spare part.

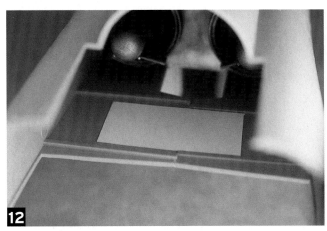

12 A sheet styrene slab reinforces the weak joint between the fuselage sides.

13 Canopies dipped in Future acrylic floor polish really gleam. John wicks away the excess polish with a cloth.

show in your paint job. I use 1800-grit paper wrapped around (ironically enough) an old 1/48 scale Phantom horizontal stabilizer to get into tight corners and crevices, **11.** Double check that you've removed all the glue marks and scratches, then shoot a few coats of Future over the model. Some scratches can actually be filled when the dry Future is sanded with fine-grit paper.

Sometimes big parts need to be reinforced at the glue joints. I epoxied a flat styrene sheet across the seam just ahead of the Phantom's engine assembly in the fuselage, **12,** and glued smaller strips over the seams in the cockpit just behind each ejection seat. This eliminated having to sand these seams away, and reduced the chances of the seams popping apart.

It's very clear. Big aircraft models have large canopies that become focal points for the viewer. Polish the windscreen and canopies, wash them in soapy water, and let them dry.

To give clear parts an extra sparkle, dip them in Future. Pour some into a bowl and dunk each clear part while holding it by a corner with a needle-nosed tweezer. If you can, leave the excess sprue on the part and use it as a handle.

Remove the immersed parts from the Future bath slowly to minimize air bubbles. Carefully wick the excess Future from the parts by running a clean cloth around the edges, **13.** Park the clear parts on toothpicks, cover them with a bowl to keep the dust off, and let the Future cure for two days.

REFERENCES
. . . And Kill MiGs Lou Drendel, Squadron/Signal Publications, Carrollton, Texas, 1997
F-4 Phantom II in Detail & Scale, USAF F-4E and F-4G Bert Kinzey, Tab Books, Blue Ridge Summit, Pennsylvania, 1982
McDonnell F-4 Phantom, Spirit in the Skies Jon Lake, Aerospace Publishing, London, England, 1992
Phantom, A Legend in Its Own Time Francis K. Mason, Motorbooks International, Osceola, Wisconsin, 1984

SOURCES
Decals Eagle Strike Productions, 2025 SW 22nd Terrace, Miami, FL 33145, fax 305-285-7219, www.EagleStrikeProductions.com
Seam scraper Micro-Mark, 340 Snyder Ave., Berkeley Heights, NJ 07922-1595, 908-464-6764, www.micromark.com
Frisket film several brands and tack-strengths available in art-supply stores
Epoxy look for clear five-minute epoxy in hardware stores
Future acrylic floor polish available in grocery stores
Super-fine sandpapers and pads available in auto-paint stores

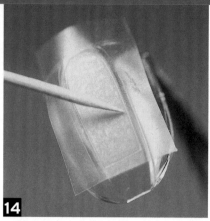

14

Frisket film burnished with a toothpick is John's favorite canopy mask.

15

The leading edges of the kit parts were painted aluminum first, then covered with the camouflage colors.

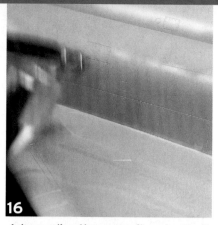

16

John applies the camouflage in small vertical strokes, simulating the application on the real aircraft. This method creates slight streaks in the paint, aiding in a convincing finish.

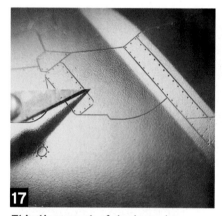

17

This tiny speck of dust can be removed by gently sanding and recoating with Future before the final flat coat is applied.

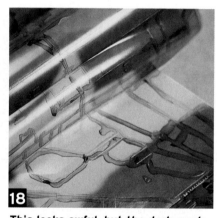

18

This looks awful, but the dark wash that flows into the panel lines will be preserved once the excess is wiped away.

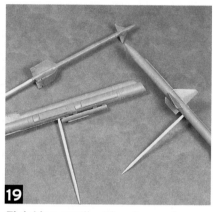

19

Finishing small underwing parts can be tricky: How do you hold them? John drills holes where they won't be visible later, then inserts toothpick handles.

Large canopies demand crisply painted frames. I recommend masking the clear areas with frisket film burnished on with a sharp toothpick, **14**. Burnishing produces better contact with the surface, keeps the masks from lifting, and makes cutting along the frame lines with a sharp blade easier. Frisket leaves less residue on Future-coated clear surfaces than other masking mediums.

Before you paint the canopy frames, trim off any sprue stubs and clean up the attachment points. The frisket masks will protect the clear areas during this process.

After painting the canopy frames, gloss them once again with Future. When they are dry, apply a clear flat coat and remove the masks. If you need to use plastic polish to remove excess masking residue, the Future and flat coats will keep the paint from rubbing off.

Finish. Large-scale aircraft models should show some wear; since everything is bigger, wear should be more evident. The bigger the model, the more realistic the wear must look.

The aircraft I chose to model is a USAF F-4E that was painted in Vietnam camouflage. Brig. Gen. Steve Ritchie, an ace pilot, flew the jet on a 1997 commemorative tour. While the paint scheme on the actual aircraft was immaculate, I produced typical wear to demonstrate finishing techniques.

You can't produce a realistically worn paint scheme by being sloppy with the paint job. Realism starts with a clean surface. Wash the entire model with soapy water and a toothbrush to get out all the sanding dust from corners and panel lines. Dry the model with a hair dryer (not too hot!).

Before applying the four-color camouflage, I prepared the model with a coat of Testor Aluminum Plate Metalizer on the leading and trailing edges of the wings and tail, the intakes and splitters, and the underwing items, **15**. I followed that with a protective coat of Future. Next I applied the camouflage with Testor's enamels. I painted the fuselage in random vertical strokes to produce a subtle, streaky appearance that adds realism to the model, **16**.

After applying each camouflage color, I lightly sanded the leading and trailing edges and the other areas with a 2400-grit sanding pad to reveal the aluminum undercoat. I used a back-and-forth motion here to simulate wear. I applied several light coats of Future to protect each color, so if I made a mistake, I could simply wipe off the newly applied paint with a little thinner without marring the underlying color.

Should you find any dust and dirt on your model at this point, **17**, don't panic. Simply wait until the Future is dry, sand the dust away with a fine-grit paper, and then regloss. Doing this after each color produces a smooth surface for applying a wash and decals.

Panel line wash. Large aircraft have lots of surface details that just cry out to be seen, so I help them out by applying a wash after the paint job is dry and glossed. I use my thinned gloss acrylic wash and slather it over the panel lines, **18**. When the wash is dry, I wipe away the excess with a clean T-shirt.

Large aircraft carry large underwing ordnance, too. To make painting these items easier, I drill small holes in inconspicuous places and insert toothpicks to serve as handles, **19**. Clothespins hold the toothpicks while the parts dry.

Decaling comes next. I used Eagle Strike's sheet No. 32010 for this aircraft, **20**. When the decals had dried, I examined the model and wiped off water spots with a damp rag, then applied another coat of Future. I sanded stubborn water spots out of decal adhesive stains with 2400-grit paper and shot another coat of Future. The last coat was clear flat (for a flat finish).

This Phantom is now ready for its parking spot—if I can find one big enough for it.

20

The Eagle Strike decals represent a commemorative Phantom from 1997, painted in Vietnam camouflage.

Ritchie's commemorative Phantoms

As a captain in 1972, Steve Ritchie flew a Phantom and was the only USAF pilot during the Vietnam war with five victories over North Vietnam MiGs. (There were two back-seater aces, Chuck DeBellevue, Ritchie's usual partner who had six victories, and Jeff Feinstein with five.)

During the U.S. Air Force's 50th anniversary celebrations in 1997, an F-4E was refurbished to represent one of Ritchie's Phantoms. At the Nellis Air Force Base, Nevada, 50th anniversary air show, Brig. Gen. Ritchie flew the commemorative Phantom for thousands of appreciative onlookers.

That aircraft is the subject of John Adelmann's model. The aircraft was originally drawn from service with the 20th Fighter Squadron at Holloman Air Force Base, New Mexico. It was painted in the standard 1970s camouflage comprising Light Gray FS 36222 undersurfaces with Tan FS 30219, Green FS 34102, and Dark Green FS 34079 upper surfaces.

Another Phantom, an F-4D (serial number 65-0749), was obtained by the Collings Foundation and refinished to represent the Phantom that Ritchie and DeBellevue used for three of their victories. The original aircraft (serial number 66-7463) is displayed at the USAF Academy in Colorado Springs, Colorado. The Collings bird displays the five stars that were painted on the left splitter plate of the original and is currently based at Ellington Field, near Houston, Texas. Ritchie also flew this restored Phantom.

- Paul Boyer

The subject of John Adelmann's model, this F-4E Phantom II was displayed at the Nellis AFB USAF 50th anniversary air show and flown by Steve Ritchie. Shawn Carroll photo

CHAPTER EIGHTEEN

Fast FAC
Ground-attack Tomcat

CONVERTING REVELL'S F-14D SUPER TOMCAT INTO AN F-14B "SMART BOMBER"

It seems strange to see a Tomcat toting bombs, but the venerable F-14 is proving to be a capable ground-attack platform. *FSM* photos by Jim Forbes and Darren Roberts.

Until recently, the F-14 Tomcat was purely an air-superiority fighter, but the

Navy has transformed it into a multi-mission airplane. Its new tasks include

night attack, reconnaissance, and fast forward air control (FAC) missions.

Shave off round radar display and replace with square multi-function display

1

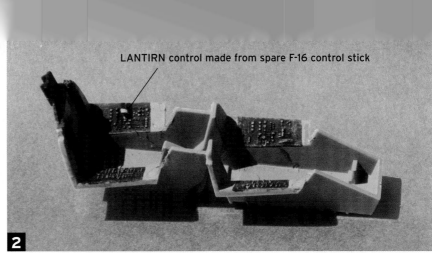

LANTIRN control made from spare F-16 control stick

2

Revell F-14D MACES seat

Monogram F-14A GRU-7 seat (good for F-14B)

3

By Darren Roberts

With the retirement of the venerable A-6 Intruders, the all-weather attack duties are shared by specially equipped F-18 Hornets and F-14 Tomcats. How do you make a Tomcat a smart bomber? The key is the LANTIRN pod (for Low-Altitude Navigation and Targeting Infra-Red at Night). It combines infrared sighting with a designator for laser-guided bombs (LGBs).

The first fleet squadron to be deployed with these capabilities was VF-103 "Jolly Rogers." Formerly the "Sluggers," VF-103 took on its new nickname in early 1996 when the original "Jolly Rogers," VF-84, was disestablished. VF-103 was first assigned to CVW-17 operating aboard the USS *Enterprise*, but has since transferred to the USS *Dwight D. Eisenhower*.

VF-103 flies the improved F-14B, which has attributes of the F-14A and D. I converted Revell's F-14D Super Tomcat back to B standards. Since the Revell model is closer to a B than a D (it's a modified Monogram F-14A), the conversion was not difficult.

Cockpit. The F-14B has basically the same instrument layout as the F-14A, which is what the Revell kit gives you. A couple of changes need to be made in the rear cockpit. Cut away the round scope and replace it with a square multi-function display,

LANTIRN pod on modified fairing

Squared-off engine fairing

4

1. I used one from the Teknics radar-display photoetched set. Also, place a control stick on the left console. This controls the laser-designator in the LANTIRN pod. It's similar to the F-16 control stick, so I used one from a Minicraft 1/48 scale F- 16, **2.**

The Revell kit provides the new

New taller UHF/TACAN antenna

5

SOURCES
Photoetched instrument panels Teknics, Meteor Productions, P.O. Box 3956, Merrifield, VA 22116, 703-971-0500
Decals SuperScale International, available from Squadron Mail Order, 1115 Crowley Drive, Carrollton, TX 75011-5010, 972-242-8663
Sheet plastic Plastrct, 1020 S. Wallace Place, City of Industry, CA 91748, 626-912-7016

REFERENCES
Aviation Week and Space Technology June 10, 1996, July 1, 1996, McGraw Hill, New York, New York
F-14 Tomcat Walkaround Lou Drendel, Squadron/Signal Publications, Carrollton, Texas, 1995
The Hook Winter 1996 and Summer 1997, Tailhook Association, San Diego, California

Bomb racks on forward Phoenix pallets

Radar-warning antenna

EMC bumps

6

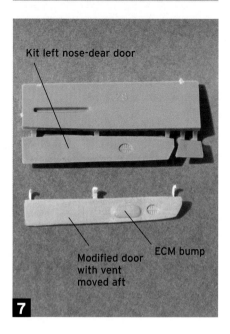

Kit left nose-dear door

ECM bump

Modified door with vent moved aft

7

NACES seats, but the F-14B has the old GRU-7 seats. I borrowed a pair from an old Monogram F-14A, but you also could use aftermarket resin seats, **3**.

Engine fairings. With the installation of new F101 engines, the fairings at the outside ends of the fuselage need to be squared off. Revell gives the original rounded fairings. To fix them, start by cutting away the horizontal stabilizers—they get in the way of the modifications. Remove the rounded fairings, then build squared-off fairings from .020" sheet styrene, **4**. Smooth the splice with putty and sandpaper, then replace the horizontal stabilizers.

Antennas and chin pod. Cut a taller dorsal UHF/TACAN antenna from sheet styrene and replace the one right behind the canopy, **5**.

I used parts from spare kits to produce the ECM bumps on the intakes, but you could shape them from styrene, **6**. The same goes for the radar-warning antennas on the wing gloves; I stole mine from an F-16 kit.

There's another ECM bump on the left nose-gear door, but before adding it, the engraved vent must be moved back. I cut apart the gear door, then placed the section with the vent to the rear and replaced the missing section with .040" sheet styrene, **7**. The ECM bump was fashioned from scrap styrene. Also, the antenna on the right nose-gear door should be removed.

The under-nose pod on the F-14B has a Television Sensor Unit (TVSU). I replaced Revell's double-barreled pod with a leftover from a Hasegawa F-14. This was glued on after all seams were filled and sanded.

Zuni and LANTIRN pods. The kit's underwing pylons need to be modified to carry the LANTIRN and Zuni pods. Cut away and discard the lower section of each Revell pylon (with the molded-on Sparrow missile).

New lower sections can be shaped from styrene, or you could modify Phoenix wing pylons from a Hasegawa kit. That's what I used. The pointed Phoenix pylon section is too long, so I cut ⅛" out of the middle

Laser-guided bombs   Four-round Zuni pod   Modified wing pylon

8

LANTIRN pod   Four-round Zuni pod

9

of each, rejoined the remaining pieces, then mounted it upside down to the top part of the Revell pylon, **8**. I armed my Tomcat for both the "fast FAC" and ground-attack missions. The left wing pylon carries a four-round Zuni rocket pod from an old Fujimi TA-4J kit (Hasegawa's weapons set No. 48-2 also has them). The LANTIRN pod on the right pylon came from a Minicraft/Academy F-15E kit, **9**.

The laser-guided bombs came from Hasegawa's weapons set No. 48-2. These were mounted to a pair of bomb racks robbed from Hasegawa's "Bombcat" kit (SP122) and placed under the forward fuselage Phoenix pallets.

Borrowed decals. After coating my Tomcat with Testor Model

Master Light Ghost Gray paint (FS36375), I masked and sprayed the antiglare panel and the tips of the tails flat black.

The VF-103 Jolly Rogers scheme has had several variations: some with black tails and white skull and crossbones, some with gray tails (with black tips) and black skull and crossbones. I chose the latter but there were no decals for it. I copied SuperScale sheet No. 48-512, since it has the last VF-84 markings, onto clear decal paper. This changes the dark gray markings to black, which is what I needed for this machine. Since the skull and crossbones are white on this sheet, I used the black ones from SuperScale No. 48-327. The AA with the lightning bolt on the insides of the tails came from SuperScale No. 72-342. Th USS *Enterprise* labels on the wing gloves came from SuperScale No. 48-328.

I sprayed the ventral fins white, and when the paint was dry, I masked the edges and painted the rest flat black. The VF-103 legends were pieced together from SuperScale No. 72-229. When the decals were dry, I overcoated with Testor Dullcote.

You often see aircraft at air shows with FOD (Foreign Object Damage) covers on the jet intakes. VF-103's covers repeated the chevrons-on-stripe motif of the fuselage band. I made covers from masking tape, **10**.

Lay tape onto an expendable surface and cut two strips 2.5cm wide and 7cm long. Paint the squadron colors (according to photos of the aircraft you are modeling) and allow them to dry. Make two small cuts 4mm from one end, then pull the tape from the surface. Fold the sides over (about 1mm to 2mm, sticky side in).

Place the top of the cover on the top of the intake front and drape it over the opening. Secure the bottom with a drop or two of super glue. Wrap the tabs at the top of the cover under the front edge of the intake and secure them with super glue. If you want the covers on permanently, don't trust the stickum of the tape—rely on super glue instead.

The covers were held on with lines pinned into small securing points on the intakes. Use fine black thread for the lines and paint the securing points silver.

That's the finishing touch. Now the latest modification of the Tomcat can join my collection. It sure looks funny carrying bombs, though, doesn't it?

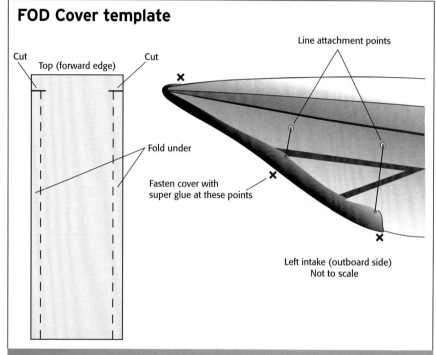

FOD Cover template

Cut

Top (forward edge)

Cut

Line attachment points

Fold under

Fasten cover with super glue at these points

Left intake (outboard side)
Not to scale

10

CHAPTER NINETEEN

U.S. Military Aircraft Colors

THE MOSTLY GRAY WORLD OF MODERN AIRCRAFT FINISHES 1955-2001

By Paul Boyer

Military aircraft camouflage colors have used the entire color spectrum since their development in World War I. Then, the German pre-printed fabric "lozenge" of colorful shades seemed to defy logic, but at a distance, the "camouflage" was effective. Later, hand-applied paints were chosen to help conceal aircraft on the ground, or to help flying aircraft blend into the background of the sky.

These two areas dictated nearly all future aircraft camouflage. In World War II, camouflaging aircraft on the ground from enemy aerial marauders produced predominantly green paint jobs. The verdant combat theatres of Europe and the Pacific featured airfields on woods' edges, so the green colors helped hide aircraft.

As the Allies gained air superiority late in the war, the extra weight of camouflage paint and the effort to maintain it became unnecessary. By 1944, most U.S. land-based planes were delivered and operated in natural metal.

Unpainted aircraft were the norm for the U.S. Air Force up to the mid-1960s. Then, camouflage was needed to blend combat aircraft into the tropical landscape of Southeast Asia. The lessons learned from that war were incorporated into many of the paint schemes on aircraft today. Browns and greens hide aircraft against certain terrain when seen from above, but do little to confuse enemy fighter pilots engaged in combat.

During the 1970s, colors were designed to confound both enemy pilots' vision and the sensors of guided missiles. The F-15's original "air-superiority blue," so highly touted as the ultimate camouflage, was too easy to see in both visual and infrared wavelengths. The solution came in a variety of "low-vis" grays that are not only difficult to see at a distance, but also absorb infrared energy.

The Naval side. Navy requirements are different, however. Nearly all carrier-based aircraft (and water-based seaplanes, floatplanes, and flying boats) are painted to protect them from corrosion caused by exposure to salty sea air.

Navy color schemes evolved from gray, to blue, and back to gray during World War II and into the 1950s. This apparent fickleness was due to the need to hide aircraft against sea surface or the sky, depending on the threat. Was it a coincidence that the gull-gray and white schemes of the late '50s through the '70s made an aircraft look like a seagull against the deep blue sea?

Current U.S. Navy aircraft colors are in accordance with the U.S. Air Force air-superiority philosophy of hiding the aircraft from enemy eyes during air combat.

What's in a name? While modelers nearly always want to identify a certain color by using a name, this practice has produced problems as military color standards change. For example, the olive drab of World War II is not the same as today's olive drab. Even the model-paint manufacturers can become confused! There are so many grays in use now that it is difficult to understand what color light gray really is. So, to get the right paint colors, modelers are better off identifying and matching them using their official five-digit Federal Standard number.

What is "FS 595?" The current U.S. government color standard is known as "Federal Standard 595b." The document and paint chips are available in three forms: loose-leaf notebook pages, 3 x 5 cards, and a fan-deck (like chips from a paint store—most convenient for modelers). There are hundreds of colors in the standard, but only a few dozen are pertinent to modelers.

A quick overview of the numbering system tells you a lot about the colors. The first digit of a five-digit FS color number denotes the sheen of the paint: 1 = glossy, 2 = semigloss, 3 = flat. The second digit describes the color "family": 0 = browns, 1 = reds, 2 = oranges, 3 = yellows, 4 = greens, 5 = blues, 6 = grays, 7 = others (blacks, whites, and metallics), and 8 = fluorescents. The last three digits are specific to the individual color and have

FS #	Common name	Gunze Aqueous	Humbrol Enamel	Polly Scale	Tamiya Color	Testor Enamel	Testor Acryl	Xtracolor Enamel	Comments
FS 30118	Field drab		142	505252	XF59	1702	4708	X101	"Snake" and "Lizard" scheme aggressors
FS 30140	Brown special			505240		2108			"Asia Minor" schemes, Gulf War Pave Low/Pave Hawk
FS 30219	Dark tan	H310	118	505392	XF52	1742	4709	X102	Brown of the "Standard" or "Southeast Asia" scheme
FS 20400	Tan special		63	505386		2021	4697	X145	"Asia Minor" schemes, Gulf War Pave Low/Pave Hawk
FS 31136	Insignia red	H327	153	414128	XF7	1705	4714	X103	Blood red used on full-color insignias
FS 12197	International orange					2022	4682	X104	Conspicuity and arctic markings after 1970, Navy trainers
FS 33531	Sand	H313	121		XF57	1706	4720	X105	"Snake," "lizard," and Israeli schemes
FS 13538	Chrome yellow	H329	188			1707	4683	X106	Trainers
FS 33538	Insignia yellow		154	505220	XF3	1708	4721	X106	Orange-yellow propeller tip, rescue and warning markings
FS 33613	Radome tan	H318	148			1709	4722	X107	Radomes and dielectric panels
FS 13655	Blue Angels yellow		69	414215	X8	2023	4684	X108	Bright yellow
FS 34031	U.S. Army helo drab					2024	4723	X153	Dark olive brown, almost black
FS 34079	Dark green	H309	116	505388	XF27	1710	4726	X110	Dark green of the "Standard" or "Southeast Asia," SAC's "SIOP," and "Asia Minor" schemes
FS 34086	Green drab					1787	4727		"Strategic" scheme B-52, B-1, FB-111A
FS 34087	Olive drab	H304	155	505370	XF62	1711	4728	X111	Army helicopters and aircraft
FS 34092	European I dark green	H302	149	505246	XF58	1764	4729	X114	A-10s, transports, helicopters
FS 34097	Field green	H340	105			1712		X115	Marine helicopters (overall or with FS 35237 and flat black)
FS 34102	Medium green	H303	117	505390	XF5	1713	4734	X116	Light green of the "Standard" or "Southeast Asia" & "European I" schemes
FS 34151	Interior green		151	505096		1715	4736	X117	Early cockpit interior color, out of use by 1960
FS 34159	SAC bomber green				XF65	1793		X118	Blue green of SAC's "SIOP" scheme
FS 34201	SAC bomber tan				XF49	1792		X119	Green-tan of SAC's "SIOP" scheme
FS 34227	Pale green	H312	120	505288		1716	4739	X148	Israeli upper-surface green (early jets)
FS 34258	Green			505310		2029		X120	"Snake" scheme aggressors
FS 35044	Insignia blue	H326	189	414230		1719	4742	X122	Used for insignias, some lettering, and cheatlines
FS 15050	Blue Angel blue	H328	190		X3	1772	4687	X123	Closest FS equivalent to automotive blue used on the Blue Angels
FS 35109	Blue					2031		X124	AT-38 "Cloud" scheme
FS 35237	Medium gray (blue-gray)	H337	145			1721	4746	X126	Topsides early Navy "Tactical Paint" Scheme, antiglare panels, camouflaged Marine helicopters
FS 35414	Blue			505318	XF23	2033		X127	"Grape" scheme aggressors
FS 35622	Duck egg blue	H314	122	505396	XF66	1722	4748	X149	Aggressor and Israeli undersurfaces
FS 16081	Navy gloss gray	H339				1791	4691	X129	"Engine gray," overall color of Navy helicopters
FS 36081	European I gray	H301	32	505204	XF63	1788	4750	X129	Dark charcoal gray of "European I" scheme on A-10s and on "Strategic" scheme B-52, B-1, and FB-111A
FS 36118	Gunship gray	H305	125	505382	XF50	1723	4752	X130	Current overall color of Air Combat Command aircraft, light gray of Strategic scheme, European I transports
FS 36173	Air Mobility Command gray		156		XF53	2035		X158	Current overall color of USAF transports
FS 36176	Dark gray F-15			505232		2036	4754	X157	Dark gray of F-15 "Mod Eagle" scheme
FS 36231	Dark gull gray	H317	140	505378	XF19	1740	4755	X131	Modern cockpit walls, floors, etc.
FS 36251	Navy aggressor gray					1794		X132	Navy aggressors, USAF "Ghost" aggressor scheme, light gray of F-15 "Mod Eagle" scheme
FS 36270	Neutral gray	H306	126	505384	XF20	1725	4754	X133	Typical standard color of F-16 radomes
FS 36307	Light sea gray		141		XF12	1726	4759	X134	"Ghost" scheme aggressors
FS 36320	Dark ghost gray	H307	128	505374		1741	4761	X135	Upper color of modern F-14, F-18, EA-6B, etc.
FS 36375	Light ghost gray	H308	127	505376		1728	4762	X136	Under-side color of modern fighters
FS 16440	Gloss light gull gray	H315	183		XF20	1729	4692	X137	Navy transports, overall color of pre-TPS Navy aircraft
FS 36440	Light gull gray	H325	129	505380	XF20	1730	4763	X137	With gloss white, standard U.S. Navy upper-surface color, 1955-1971
FS 16473	Aircraft gray	H57	146		XF66	1731	4693	X138	Transports and interceptors ("ADC gray"): a flat version (FS 36473) used on FAC O-2 and OV-10A
FS 36492	Light gray					2038		X147	Light gray on EF-111A and EC-130
FS 36495	Light gray	H338	147	505280	XF14	1732	4765	X139	Under-side gray on early F-18s and some adversary F-18s
FS 16515	"Canadian Voodoo grey"					2039		X150	"707 gray," "Boeing gray" used on E-3 Sentry and E-8 JSTARS, late C-9 Nightingale
FS 36622	Camouflage gray	H311	28	505394		1733	4766	X140	Under-side color of "Standard" or "Southeast Asia" and "Asia Minor" schemes
FS 28913	Fluorescent red-orange		209			2041			High-visibility color for transports, trainers, and helicopters, 1960-1970
FS 28915	Fluorescent orange	H98	193			1775	4703		High-visibility color for transports, trainers, 1958-1960

Standard Camouflage Schemes

This list specifies the colors used for standard camouflage schemes. Not all aircraft were painted in the "standard" schemes. Some variations occurred due to application error or substitute colors.

Air Combat Command gray: Overall FS 36118 (F-15E, B-1B, B-2A)
Air Mobility Command gray: Overall FS 36173 (C-17, C-5, KC-10, KC-135, C-130)
European I (transports and helicopters): FS 36118, FS 34102, FS 34092 (C-130, C-141, C-5, H-3)
European I (attack aircraft): FS 36081, FS 34102, FS 34092 (A-10)
European I (other attack): FS 36081, FS 34079 (A-37B, A-7D)
European I (fighters): FS 36081, FS 34102, FS 34079 (F-4D/E/G)
Ghost scheme (Compass Ghost): FS 36320 and FS 36375 (F-14, F-15, F-18, EA-6B, A-10, SH-3, SH-60)
Mod Eagle scheme: FS 36176 and FS 36251 (F-15, F-22)
Hill Gray II: FS 36118 tops over FS 36270 bottoms and sides (late F-4E/G, F-16)
Asia Minor scheme: FS 20400, FS 30140, FS 34079, FS 36622 undersurfaces
Modified Asia Minor scheme: FS 20400, FS 30140 (MH-53J, MH-60)
Standard camouflage: FS 30219, FS 34102, FS 34079 over FS 36622 undersurfaces (most Vietnam War-era aircraft)
Modified standard camouflage: FS 30219, FS 34102, FS 34079 over gloss black undersurfaces (F-111)
SAC Single Integrated Operations Plan (SIOP) scheme: FS 34201, FS 34159, FS 34079 over gloss white
  (B-52, FB-111A; most B-52s had gloss black undersurfaces)
SAC "Strategic" scheme: FS 36081, FS 36118, FS 34086 (B-52, FB-111A, B-1B)
U.S. Navy Tactical Paint Scheme (TPS): Varies, but usually similar to Ghost scheme. Early variations included FS 35237 tops (F-14, A-6, A-7, SH-3)
Harrier: FS 36118 top, FS 36231 sides, FS 36320 bottom
U.S. Navy helicopters (some current): FS 16081 (CH-46) or gloss white over FS 16440 (SH-3)
U.S. Marines helicopters: FS 34097 overall or with FS 37038 (flat black), and FS 35237 camouflage (CH-46, CH-53)
USAF electronic: FS 36320 over FS 36492 (EF-111A, EC-130)
USAF trainers: Gloss white uppersurfaces over FS 15044 (gloss insignia blue) undersurfaces (T-37)
U.S. Navy/Marine trainers: FS 12197 areas on overall gloss white (T-45, TA-4J, T-34C)

a lot to do with light reflectivity and other scientific stuff that we don't need to worry about.

You should note that some colors can be found in different finishes and differ only in that sheen. For example, the glossy FS 16081 (unofficially called "engine gray") is the same shade as the flat FS 36081 ("European I gray").

Do you need a copy of the government color standards? No, unless you want or need to mix your own colors. In today's modeling world, nearly all modern U.S. aircraft colors are available premixed by at least one model-paint manufacturer. While you don't need the actual chips, it is valuable to know which color is which and on what aircraft it is used. We hope this chart helps you.

Available modeling paints. Model paints come and go (and so do some paint manufacturers). This chart shows modern U.S. aircraft colors and what model paints can be found to match them. I did not include blacks, whites, and metallics in this

A McDonnell Douglas F/A-18C Hornet of FVA-136 wears the typical ghost gray scheme of FS 36320 uppersurfaces and FS 36375 undersurfaces. DOD photo

This LTV A-7D Corsair II of the 23rd TFW wears a bicentennial band on the tail. The wrap-around camouflage is FS 30219, FS 34102, and FS 34079. DOD photo

table. If your kit instructions recommend a certain brand that you can't get, you can use the chart to determine what other brands you can use.

Thanks to the Testor Corp., whose data formed the basis of this chart.

CHAPTER TWENTY

Refurbishing AMT's B-52H

FIXING AND MODERNIZING THE LATE-MODEL BUFF

Big, bad, and bodacious, Boeing's bomber beats beautiful but boring beasts beyond belief. If that's too many Bs for your bonnet, try resurrecting AMT's Stratofortress kit sometime! *FSM*'s Senior Editor shows you how.

I have been holding on to a couple of AMT/Ertl 1/72 scale B-52 kits for several years now, just waiting to get in the mood to build one. Getting in the mood was key because I knew there were problems with the kit.

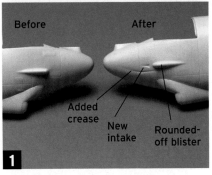

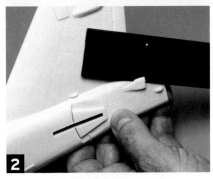

Before After

Added crease

New intake

Rounded-off blister

1

Small changes were made to the model's nose. Paul added a subtle crease along the radome hinge line, refined the ECM bumps, and added air scoops.

2

The early-style ECM fairings near the tail had to go, so they were cut away with a razor saw.

By Paul Boyer
Photos by Jim Forbes and
William Zuback

I first had to determine what my level of satisfaction would be. Did I want to correct every inaccuracy? Smooth over every fit problem? Invent a way to realistically droop the wings? Upgrade the airframe's equipment to current fit? How about markings? Agh! Too much to think about.

Until now.

When I remembered that the 50th anniversary of the B-52's first flight was this past spring, I started looking at books and articles about the venerable old BUFF and became energized to do something with that big box of plastic.

Whenever I take on a modeling project, I consider whether it would be of interest to *FSM* readers. "I'll bet a lot of them would like to know how

to make something halfway decent from this monster," I figured. So why not fix some of the more glaring problems and upgrade the kit into a current B-52H from Operation Enduring Freedom?

What you get. The kit comes as a B-52H from the late 1980s, with the EVS turrets under the nose, the rear fuselage extension, Phase VI ECM bumps, and air-launched cruise missiles mounted on the underwing pylons (even though it is missing the leading-edge wing-root fairings that were supposed to be installed on cruise-missile carriers in accordance with the SALT II agreements).

To make it into an Operation Enduring Freedom B-52H, I had to reconfigure the ECM antennas slightly, remove the tail gun, find current underwing bombs and pylons, and obtain up-to-date markings. And then, of course, fix the kit's problems.

Up here. The overall shape of the nose is pretty good, but some details are missing and some are overstated. A prominent crease is missing along the horizontal edge of the hinged, one-piece radome. The crease swings upward going forward until it smoothes out toward the nose tip. I used files to gouge the soft plastic, and sanding sticks to smooth the area, **1**. The ECM blister on the side of the nose was too sharp, so I rounded it off with sanding sticks. Small NACA-style scoops should be right in front of the blisters, but they

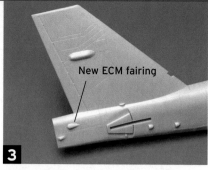

3

New rounded ECM fairings were made from the kit's fat sprue and shaped with sanding sticks.

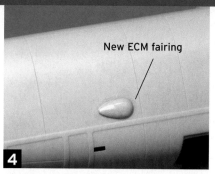

4

Additional streamlined ECM fairings were added to the rear fuselage, cut and shaped from the kit sprue.

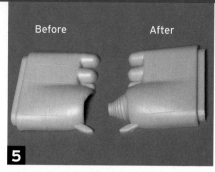

5

Current BUFFs have had their tail guns removed. Paul scored around the "flexible" tail stinger and removed it.

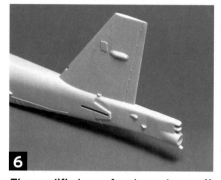

6

The modified rear fuselage shows off the new ECM fairings and the covered gun station. The tail ends of the fuselages have been extended to house more ECM gear.

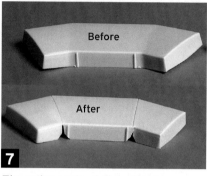

7

The outer ends of the wing box were bent downward by cutting wedges out of the sides and scoring the top.

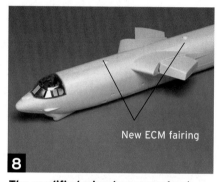

8

The modified wing box was glued into the assembled fuselage. Note the added teardrop-shaped fairings on top of the fuselage and the foil-masked windows.

were missing, so I carved them out with a blade.

The EVS blisters fit poorly onto the bottom of the nose. Gap-filling super glue worked great here. I just poured it in and let it run into the seams. There were a couple of strange blade antennas sticking out from each side of the nose. I think they were supposed to be pitot tubes, but I removed them. The NACA scoops along the bottom of the fuselage sides were ill defined, so I enhanced them with the blade.

I didn't attempt to detail the cockpit; I just used the kit parts. The instrument panel decal in the kit is about 25 percent bigger than the plastic panel, so save yourself some frustration and don't use it. Just paint the raised detail on the kit panel. The canopy fit pretty well, and I masked the windows with Bare-Metal Foil.

Back there. The rear quarters of the four-piece fuselage are molded

with the vertical fin. There were several things to fix before assembly. The flat ECM antennas at the back end of the fuselage had to be cut away with a razor saw, **2**. These were replaced with a pair of teardrop blisters cut from the kit's huge sprues and shaped with sanding sticks, **3**.

Another teardrop-shaped blister needed to be added to each side of the fuselage, just behind the rear gear bays, **4**. These were also cut from the sprue and shaped with sanding sticks.

The Vulcan cannon tail stinger has been removed from the B-52H fleet, so I cut mine out by scoring around the "flexible" cone molding with a sharp blade, **5**. After I joined the halves, I covered the resulting hole with .010" sheet styrene, **6**.

The fit of the front fuselage to the rear is not great. Ideally, you should glue left front to left rear, repeat for the right side, then close the completed halves while the glued joints

are still soft. Easier said than done, as you also have to align and attach the cockpit and the forward and aft gear bay interiors.

I chose instead to assemble the front halves first, then the rear halves, then join them. However, the large interior flanges at the front/rear joints didn't allow simply sliding the assemblies together. I had to cut away most of the flanges and relied on gap-filling super glue to hold the big pieces together. It worked well, and after a lot of sanding and rescribing panel lines, the joint looked pretty good.

That pesky wing box. The big bugaboo with the AMT kit is the box that helps support the wings where they attach to the fuselage. As molded, the outer ends of the box angle up slightly, and they cause the wings to sit nearly straight out. This might be fine for a flying pose, but a loaded B-52 on the ground should exhibit lots of wing droop—with the outrigger gears

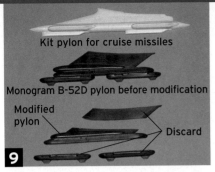

Kit pylon for cruise missiles

Monogram B-52D pylon before modification

Modified pylon

Discard

9 Paul resorted to a spare Monogram B-52D bomb pylon to make the proper stub pylons for the B-52H.

10 After the wings were glued to the fuselage, the gaps at the top of the joints were filled with strip styrene and gap-filling super glue.

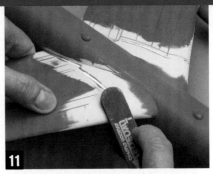

11 Paul painted the wings and fuselage before joining them, so after the filled joints were sanded smooth he rescribed panel lines and touched up.

12 The finished nose shows off the custom "Memphis Belle IV" decals and added pitot tubes and antennas.

13 Just like its World War II-vintage B-17F namesake, "Memphis Belle IV" has the Belle in a red suit on the right side of the nose, and a blue suit on the left.

14 Tail markings include the Air Combat Command badge, tail codes, and a blue band for the Barksdale AFB 2nd Bomb Wing.

touching the ground. Since that's what I wanted, I had to modify the wing box.

The box is open at the bottom, which simplified things somewhat. At the outer panel bend line, I cut notches into the front and back sides, 7. Next, I scored the top of the box along the bend lines with a blade, being careful not to cut through. With the notches cut out and the top scored, I could bend the outer panels so they were horizontal. I used liquid plastic cement and gap-filling super glue on the cut and score lines to freeze the corrected attitude.

I fed the wing box into one wing opening and out through the other, centered it, and glued it in place, 8. I let it set up a couple of days before attaching the wings.

Two more chunks from the giant sprues were used to make the large blisters on the top of the fuselage. I cut off the thick "Christmas tree"

antennas on the rear fuselage to make cleaning the seams easier. I replaced them with thinner versions after painting.

Wings. AMT's wing assemblies include the engine nacelles, weapons pylons, underwing tanks, and outriggers. The fit of the wing halves was not good, so I shaved off the alignment pins and took my time gluing the edges, adjusting the fit as I went along. I had prepainted the insides of the outrigger bays and the interior of the little doors with yellow zinc chromate.

The outrigger doors were far too thick for the scale, so I sanded them down to half the original thickness. My favorite way to sand small flat parts is to "grab" them with a hunk of sticky putty and rub them on coarse sandpaper on my workbench.

The engine nacelles were undersized, but there was no easy fix, aside from expensive and hard-to-find

resin substitutes. I went with the kit nacelles. The nacelle parts break along real panel lines, so I didn't get too fussy about eliminating seams. The underwing fuel tanks fit poorly to the wing, so I had to file away plastic and fill with sheet styrene.

Bomb pylons. The kit pylons are the streamlined ones for carrying air-launched cruise missiles. I was hoping to modify them to look like the pylons used to carry free-fall bombs, but there was no way. Instead, I modified old-style pylons from a scrapped Monogram B-52D.

First, I used a razor saw to cut away the two multiple ejector racks from the heavy stores adapter beam, then cut the beam from the Hound Dog pylon, 9. After sanding the bottom of the pylon and covering the opened top and bottom of the beam with sheet styrene, I reattached the beam slightly forward of its original position.

The pylon itself is taller than the

SOURCES
AMT's B-52H kit is out of production, but not exactly rare. Keep your eyes peeled for it on modeler Internet sites, eBay, and at model contest swap meets
JDAMs Hasegawa Aircraft Weapons VII: U.S. special bombs and LANTIRN pods (kit No. X72-12), distributed by Marco Polo Import Inc., 632 S. Coralridge Place, City of Industry, CA 91746, 626-333-2328, www.marcopoloimport.com
Self-adhesive foil Bare-Metal Foil & Hobby Co., P.O. Box 82, Farmington, MI 48332, 248-476-4366, www.bare-metal.com
Sheet and strip styrene Evergreen Scale Models, 18620-F 141st Ave. N.E., Woodinville, WA 98072, 877-376-9099

Lovingly called the BUFF (Big Ugly Fat Fellow) since at least the Vietnam era, the 50-year-old workhorse bomber still flies in combat today. B-52H models are the only ones still in service.

ones currently used, so I cut a lot off the top, using the kit pylon as a template to cut the right shape.

Weapon of choice. Joint Direct Attack Munitions (JDAMs) are free-fall iron bombs with guidance kits attached to the tails and shallow stabilizing fins on a girdle strapped around the bodies. Good examples of 2,000-pound JDAMs can be found in Hasegawa's Weapon Set Seven (No. X12), but you get only three in the box. I needed 12, six on each beam (the middle three racks go empty when carrying the big JDAMs). I used .040" x ⅛" styrene strip for the nine racks on each beam. I notched them so they would fit the JDAMs.

Painting. Mercifully, B-52s are painted overall FS 36118 "gunship gray" so at least this part of the project was easy. Current BUFFs have an interesting mix of landing gear colors. The wheels and struts are gloss white, while the main bays and door interiors are FS 16473 gloss "aircraft gray." The outrigger bays and door interiors are flat yellow zinc chromate.

I painted the fuselage and wings separately before mounting the wings. This made it easier to get into tight areas such as the inboard sides of the engine pylons.

The moment of truth. Joining the wings to the fuselage was tricky. The modified wing box allowed me to establish the correct attitude of the wings, but didn't automatically set it. I slid the wings onto the box and glued the bottom seams with liquid cement. With the main landing gear and wheels mounted in the fuselage, and the outriggers planted in the wings, I placed the model on a large table and let the wheels touch ground all around. This "jig" set the proper droop to the wings while the bottom joints set up.

Now all that was needed was to fill and sand the top seams. The modified wing box allowed the wings to droop, but opened the top seams quite a bit. I stuffed pieces of styrene strips into the gaps and glued them in place, **10**. When the joint was dry, I shaved away the excess plastic, filled remaining gaps with gap-filling super glue, and sanded the areas smooth, **11**. Several panel lines had to be rescribed, but after that, quick retouching with the airbrush was enough to hide the seams.

The next step was an overall gloss coat of Future floor polish. Future not only supplied a smooth surface for decals, but also helped protect the paint finish from handling as I finished the model. The gloss coat also

allowed me to apply a flat black "sludge wash" (see Nov. 2001 FSM).

Special markings. When I made my model, no aftermarket decals were available for an Operation Enduring Freedom BUFF. The one I wanted to depict was "Memphis Belle IV," the first B-52H built, and therefore the oldest B-52 in service. It flew several missions over Afghanistan flying from Diego Garcia in the Indian Ocean. I was able to have Juanita Franzi's fine profile artwork printed onto clear decal paper in scale on an Alps printer. I hope a decal company makes the markings for this one soon.

The custom markings were on both sides of the nose, **12** and **13** (note how the "Belle" is printed in blue on one side, and red on the other, just like its World War II B-17F namesake). Tail markings include codes, the serial number, and the blue Barksdale Air Force Base band at the tip, **14**.

I used dark gull gray decal stripes to define the walkways on the fuselage, wing, and tailplanes.

Final touches. The last steps included adding all of the small fragile antennas and pitot tubes. I used thin sheet styrene for these, copying the thick kit parts where I could. Finally, a clear flat coat evened the overall finish. I fashioned the twin anticollision beacons in front of the fin from clear-red-painted drops of gap-filling super glue on foil.

Thar 'tis. Making AMT's B-52H look halfway decent wasn't half bad! Now I just need a half-acre to park it!